# From Lemons to Lemonade

# From Lemons to Lemonade

## 47 Sweet Lessons from Life

Glenda Haskell

June 6, 2018

For Jan—

You are an artist through and through, and it's been a pleasure to see some of your gorgeous and inventive works over these years. I hope you enjoy this book, which is central to my creative spirit. Thank you!

With love and always a friend,

Glenda

Library of Congress Control Number: 2017918040
Glenda Haskell, Ann Arbor, MI


ISBN: 0999667807
ISBN 13: 9780999667804

Glenda Haskell
P.O. Box 7612
Ann Arbor, MI 48107
www.glendahaskell.com

*For my family and life learners everywhere*

# Acknowledgements

SO MANY PEOPLE to thank!

- My parents, Glenn and Dorothy Haskell, where it all began, and for trying one more time for a girl
- My loving husband of forty years, Rick Reichman, for just about everything
- Our daughters Brenna and Janelle for being the fine women they are and sources of so much inspiration (and to my son-in-law Ben for being such a good husband and father)
- My grandson Jack for being a happiness machine that never shuts off
- My two brothers Brent and Peter for always being there (and my deceased brother Brian for his truly unconditional love)
- Family members, friends, and former colleagues (some anonymous, some named) who gave me permission to include stories that involved them
- My first-round editor Jim Johnston for his faith in me and his excellent advice (especially about the chapters wisely left on the cutting-room floor)
- My line editor Anita LeBlanc, who played a significant role in making the book far better than it would have been without her expertise and guidance
- Life coach and dear friend Sallie Justice for her top-notch coaching and encouragement at many points along the way
- Other friends who provided key support along the way, including Barbaranne Branca, Pat Materka (fellow author who generously

shared numerous book publication resources), Brad Waters, and Nancy Wolff

- The many social scientists, scholars, and others whose work on understanding human motivation and behavior provides us all with a wealth of knowledge and practical guidance
- The residents of Ann Arbor and Dexter, Michigan, for supporting the fine libraries where I spent many hours working on this book
- The owners of coffee shops everywhere who give writers like me a place to work
- This splendid earth that needs us now more than ever to be good stewards
- Life itself, wonderful life. Isn't life grand?

# Table of Contents

# Introduction

*I don't know who I am*
*But you know life is for learning*

–Joni Mitchell

In August 1969, during the summer after I decided to take a break from college (which would last two-and-a-half years), the Woodstock Music Festival took place. At the time, I worked as a map scribe in Chester, Vermont, where I bent over a light table, using a tool to carefully remove road and highway stripes from the top layer of color on a large scribe sheet that would be used to print a single color of the map. Although unaware of Woodstock at the time it happened, like so many of my generation I came to love both its music and the ways the event unfolded.

In the following year, the brilliant Joni Mitchell wrote and recorded the song, "Woodstock," also memorialized in that same year by the sweet harmonies of David Crosby, Stephen Stills, Graham Nash, and Neil Young. The line above from Mitchell's song captured perfectly a conclusion I reached at that time in my life, one that has stayed with me ever since. *Life*, I decided, and as Joni's lyrics said so simply but powerfully, *is for learning*. This book is a collection of some of the many lessons I have learned in the years since, as I moved through the phases of my life.

Sometimes the best lessons come from the hardest times. For me the hardest ones came with my mother's death when I was nine, followed by, a few years later, the tough years after my father remarried up until the time I was finally able to launch my own life. As those challenging years would teach me, it's not always easy to make lemonade when life throws you lemons, at least not right away.

Fortunately, time does tend to heal, making it more possible over time to add sugar and stir. Plus, as an adult, life has given me generous portions of its sweetness, as I fell in love with and married a wonderful man and then, over the next six years, became the mother of two daughters. Professionally, I have also been lucky, as numerous supervisors and colleagues mentored and encouraged me during more than thirty years of my career in higher education, most of them at the University of Michigan.

When I began to write this book, I had no idea what a long, arduous, and meaningful journey it would be. In 2011, I brought my career in higher education to a close to, among other activities, become a trained and certified life coach and subsequently to establish my coaching business. To help me navigate these waters, I took many workshops. One I attended in 2012 focused on the potential benefits of writing a book in building a business. (At its heart, the program was a sales pitch for a "write and publish your own book" program, which I chose not to pursue, largely because of its high price tag.). Since I have always been a writer at heart, if not consistently in practice, before the end of that hour-long workshop I made a firm mental commitment to do just that.

At the time, I figured the book would be in print by the end of the year. Ha! A couple of years later, I finally stopped saying just when the book would be done. But I also knew without a doubt that I *would* finish the book and publish it, as week after week I maintained the practice of clocking the hours at coffee shops and libraries, during which I wrote, researched, and completed round after round of edits. No words can sufficiently convey how happy it makes me to be able to say, at last, "Here it is!"

Creating this book has been an organic process, as the chapters seemed to almost tumble out of me. When I finally put them all together, I was shocked to find I had penned a manuscript of more than 95,000 words. A few weeks later, with great relief I decided to peel away ten chapters, which seemed to belong more naturally to each other rather than to the rest of the book. Perhaps (I shudder to suggest) they will form the nucleus of my next book. Because I wrote the book so organically, I divided the chapters into sections only afterward, which, thankfully, seemed to work.

Although this book is comprised of stories from my life and others', I hope they will also serve as a springboard for you, my readers, to plumb your own life experiences for lessons learned. For this reason, at the end of each chapter I have given you a set of questions to ponder.

So, please pull up a chair, grab a citrus squeezer, and take the lid off the sugar bowl. Add ice and a straw, stir with a spoon (can you see the beads of moisture dripping down the outside of the cool glass?), and enjoy mixing up your own life's lemonade. Although birthing this book has been like taking many deep, satisfying dives into my own life, I also wrote it for you.

## *A note of explanation about moving to a different house midstream*

When I began work on this book early in 2012, my husband and I lived on the northeast side of Ann Arbor, Michigan in a modest cape we purchased twenty-five years earlier. Then, early in 2016, after I had completed roughly two-thirds of the book, we bought and moved into a different home in Scio Township, located an equal distance between Ann Arbor and the town of Dexter.

Because of this mid-book move, I wrote some of the chapters from the perspective of life in the "old" house (as our grandson calls it), while others took the viewpoint of life in our new home. Since the book is organized thematically rather than chronologically, my perspective as the writer has jumped back and forth between old house and new. Although I have done my best to edit the work to clarify the two different perspectives, please excuse any confusion that might arise. There's yet another lesson: while writing a book, especially one full of personal narrative, it's best to wait until after the book is done before changing houses.

I

# Letting Go

Fortune leaves always some door open to come at a remedy.

–Miguel de Cervantes, *Don Quixote*

If you wish to know how much preferable wisdom is to gold, then observe: if you change gold you get silver for it, but your gold is gone; but if you exchange one sort of wisdom for another, you obtain fresh knowledge, and at the same time keep what you possessed before.

–The Talmud

CHAPTER 1

# A Lesson in Willpower from Childhood

IN MY HOMETOWN of Springfield, Vermont, Dad worked a full-time job at Fellows Gear Shaper. In creating jobs for more than three thousand people, Gear Shaper and three other companies producing precision machinery offered good, steady work that pulled my father and many more like him to town. This was a time when for most workers, company-sponsored health insurance still belonged to the future. So, during the two years of Mom's cancer and decline, the medical bills for her care simply piled up as my father paid what he could.

After Mom died, Dad found a harsh reality staring him in the face; if he was ever going to get out of debt, he had to pick up some part-time work. For lots of reasons, this was not an easy thing to do. Although he never talked about my mother's death, my father must have been reeling emotionally from having lost her. For the two of them, just being together made for a good day. He was now a single parent to four children (Brent, Brian, and Peter—my three older brothers, and me) with all its incumbent responsibilities and worries. At eleven and nine, Peter and I were too young to fly solo.

So, in the summer of 1960, the year after Mom died, hard or not, every Saturday morning Dad got up early to drive to his second job, painting houses with his friend Larry. As for child care, he had no choice but to leave Peter and me at home. With our oldest brother in college, this responsibility fell to our slightly nutty sixteen-year-old brother Brian, which is a story unto itself. Still, he deserves a lot of credit for putting up with our shenanigans and keeping us out of harm's way. (Sadly, Brian died in 2005.)

On one of those Saturday mornings, I got it into my head that I wanted to go with my father to his house-painting job. Larry had a son about my age and there were times when we played together while my Dad and Larry painted. So shortly before Dad planned to leave, I went into his room to plead my case.

On that day, though, my father was either unable or unwilling to let me come with him. Although I was what you would call a "good kid," after he said no I threw one heck of a fit. Over and over, I pounded my fist into the rumpled sheets on Dad's unmade bed, sobbing and screaming, "I wanna go! I wanna go!" In the meantime, my father left the room, calmly closed the bedroom door behind him, climbed into the car, and drove off to work. Eventually, I wore myself out and fell asleep.

What did I do when I woke up, humbled and yes, embarrassed by my antics? I can't recall exactly, but I expect I did what kids usually did back them—headed outdoors to play. Being the man he was, my father never said a word about my little scene. No one did, including me. In his calm way, Dad told me no and stuck to it—without, much to his credit as a parent, rubbing my nose in it. For my part, I learned an important lesson. My dad had a job to do (earn some desperately-needed extra money) and I had mine (accept his answer and move on). Perhaps even more importantly, Dad trusted me to work it out.

Thinking back to my own childhood and to how my husband and I raised our two daughters, with what I like to think of as a good blend of boundaries and independence, I understand that the lesson from that Saturday morning was mostly about building willpower. As Mick Jagger sings in his memorably soulful voice, "You can't always get what you want." And though we hate to admit it at times, we know this to be a good thing. Looking back, I learned a lot from my "I-Wanna-Go" tantrum and later experiences continued to help me grow into a person with willpower muscle. Thanks, Dad.

## *Questions to Ponder*

- Can you recall at least one experience in your life when you did not get your way, and which, in the end, proved to be an opportunity for you to flex your willpower muscle?
- Have you ever found yourself wanting to "have the last word," rather than leaving well enough alone?
- Are there any helpful boundaries you would like to set for yourself?

CHAPTER 2

# Lesson from a Little Green Fingernail

ONE DAY, I was with a group of other life coaches at a coffee shop. Directly across the table from me sat Mary, whom I was meeting for the first time (not her real name). Mary had shoulder-length, wavy, brown hair that bounced when she turned her head, and tiny lines that curved from her mouth toward her brown eyes—lines surely the result of a great deal of smiling, which is what she was doing. She radiated positivity through the lilt of her voice and warm hand gestures. Right away, I liked her.

As the group's conversation meandered around various topics, my eyes were drawn again and again to something unusual about Mary. Her fingernails were painted lime green, the kind of color that makes a statement. Nine of her nails were impeccable–curved just over the tips of her fingers, well cared for, maybe even professionally manicured. (As a woman who has always kept my nails clipped short, no attention beyond a basic clipper and quick swipes of an emery board, I admire, even envy, such lovely fingernails.) What kidnapped my attention, though, was the little finger on one of her hands, considerably shorter than the others. At the tip of this finger sat an upside-down, tiny, decorative crescent moon.

What I loved about this sassy green fingernail was the way it transformed something atypical, unusual, and abnormal into something exceptional, offbeat and fun. It celebrated the very thing many of us fight against: imperfection. To acknowledge the miracle of human life, people often say newborn babies have ten perfect fingers and toes. Nine of Mary's nails were perfect, but her flawed tenth shows the world something about her character.

Most of us feel flawed in one way or another. My physical cross to bear (admittedly a relatively light one as physical imperfections go) is seborrheic keratosis, a common condition that runs in my family. SK, as I call it, manifests singly or in clusters on the skin as scaly bumps. In my case, they grow most notably on my back. (I imagine them as a group of islands on a map.) I also have a few small clusters along my hairline and on my neck, thankfully in much smaller form. (How I envy women with smooth, unblemished necks!) Although many people mistake these for potentially worrisome moles, they are not. Although a nuisance and sometimes the cause of staring eyes, they are harmless. Nevertheless, for much of my life I have taken pains not to call attention to my neck.

Enter the diamond necklace. In 1977, my mother-in-law gave me a heart-shaped diamond necklace that she'd had a jeweler create using one of her diamonds. I wore it on my wedding day. After the wedding, the necklace sat in a corner of my jewelry box, seated in the red velvet folds of a small white ring box for thirty-five years. Why? Because at the time, I found the heart-shaped setting a bit cliché. So, there it sat, the most valuable piece of jewelry I owned, unworn.

A bit serendipitously, not long before I met Mary, I withdrew the necklace from its hiding place and saw it, through new eyes, as an apt symbol of abundance, with its marriage of diamond and heart. On that day I decided, despite the risk of drawing eyes to the smattering of SK on my neck, to begin to wear it regularly. For at least a year, every day I brought the two ends of the thin gold chain around to the back of my neck to clasp them together. I made it a habit each day to touch the heart-enclosed diamond, to remind myself of abundance big and small swirling around me. Perhaps the scaly clusters on my back were invisible X's of buried treasure." Maybe the necklace is my version of Mary's tiny painted fingernail.

After our coaching group broke up, I pulled Mary aside to tell her how much I admired her special fingernail. As I left the café, I reached involuntarily to the diamond hanging around my neck, and then to my neck itself, in all its imperfection. Then, following Mary's lead, I let a smile take over my face.

## *Questions to Ponder*

- Does your body carry a physical "flaw," something you feel embarrassed about or even ashamed of?
- What would it take for you to accept it as just another part of who you are?
- Akin to Mary's decorating her fingernail or my wearing a diamond necklace, what symbolic action might you take to honor your imperfection?

CHAPTER 3

# Lessons from Being Stood Up

AT WELL PAST six o'clock on a Monday evening, the colorful salads I had prepared sat on the shelf in the refrigerator next to the marinating salmon fillets. Fresh-cut green beans waited in a casserole dish in the microwave. The table was set for two. My husband was away on his annual guys-only wilderness trip out west. Although I miss Rick while he's away, I also enjoy having the house to myself. This was one of those nights, when I looked forward to having a good friend for dinner, just the two of us. The only thing missing from this dinner party, though, was my friend. As someone who has a reputation for fretting just before an event about whether I have the right day, I double-checked my calendar and then my friend's email confirming our plans. Yes, I had the right evening.

Since this is a trusted and dependable friend, a part of me began to worry. Was she okay? To find out, I called her home, left her a voicemail message, and sent her an email. As the minutes ticked by, while I sat at the round glass table next to our tall kitchen windows, disappointment and anger wormed their way into me. As worry gave way to hurt, I dropped into a bad mood. Some people call times like this a pity party, and I was having a whopper.

*Okay*, the voice inside my head commanded, *you are going for a walk—now!* Within minutes I was out the door, locking it behind me. One of several rewards from taking a brisk walk is that we draw a lot of air into our lungs. When this happens, the brain and every other part of the body make big, helpful physiological changes. As my brain moved away from its fight-or-flight reptilian state into one that's more rational, I started to calm down.

*Would my friend ever do anything to intentionally upset me?* Not a chance. *Did I know for sure what was happening in her life at that moment?* No. At about that time, with my blood pressure well on its way back to normal, I walked by a friend's house in the neighborhood. This friend is a master gardener who has planted an eye-catching array of flowers in the flowerbeds on her double lot that fill with color from spring to fall. (Her collection of dahlias in late summer and early fall is stunning.)

I could see my garden-loving friend had had a good day. Honest dirt was wedged beneath her fingernails, smudged generously over her T-shirt, and smeared here and there on her face. Her knees reminded me of how dirty I used to get when I was a kid. She asked if I would like to have some of her garden's Siberian irises. I happily accepted her offer, and we made plans for me to come by the next morning with a plastic tub. Cheered up considerably, I continued my walk to Argo Park next to the river, along the trail through the woods, and up the hill toward home.

Back home again, still no word from my friend. But after a good walk and the treat of my gardening friend's offer, a feeling of acceptance had spread over me. I even decided to treat the evening as a kind of mini personal retreat (one of the goals I had set for myself during —the eleven days my husband would be gone.) As I became engrossed, the evening passed.

At around ten o'clock, the phone rang. Embarrassed and deeply apologetic, my friend explained that just minutes earlier she had woken up from what she intended to be a short nap before joining me for dinner. An action-packed weekend, she said, must have caught up with her, pulling her into a sleep so deep that not even my earlier phone call broke the spell. Feeling accepting, even light-hearted, about the situation (and still, I was happy to see, observing my thoughts), I laughed and assured her that I understood. We made plans for her to come the following night, an evening we both enjoyed thoroughly.

Looking back, I plumbed the experience for lessons learned. What had I done to help shift my thoughts, my mood, and my feelings toward my friend? I took physical action, an excellent way to break out of ruminating, by taking a brisk walk. It also can be useful to be deliberately mindful of the crazy-making, pesky inner voice in our heads, to acknowledge unhelpful thoughts and then picture them drifting away. Plus, there are numerous ways to uncover and challenge the irrational thinking that most of us indulge in regularly. (One of my favorite approaches is found in David Burns' *The Feeling Good Handbook.* To this day, his term "twisted thinking" brings a smile to my face.)

My bookshelves are well stocked with self-improvement books on a range of topics. Despite my reading and research, my negative inner dialogues focus all too easily on worst-case scenarios and are just as ingrained as the next person's. On this night, though, I managed to combine a few tricks to dig myself out of the usual rut and into the light of (a more rational) perspective.

A few weeks later, it was my turn to miss an appointment with a different friend in an event I call "what goes around comes around." We had planned a phone date, as my friend needed to be at home and couldn't meet me in person. Even though I didn't have a single excuse to stand on, my friend was generous in her understanding and forgave me quickly.

What a good thing it is when we can bring ourselves to the point of embracing other people (and ourselves) as flawed, imperfect beings. So, here's a toast to remembering to vigilantly keep up the good fight against our negative irrational thinking and to being more compassionate and forgiving. The good news is that with the right attitude and frame of mind, the supply of these key ingredients to a happy life knows no bounds.

## *Questions to Ponder*

- Can you think of a time when a friend "stood up" or disappointed you?
- Can you think of a time when you "stood up" or disappointed a friend?
- What are the life lessons you might harvest from these experiences?
- What's one thing you could do in these kinds of circumstances to show compassion not only to others, but also to yourself?

CHAPTER 4

# Lessons from Not Delivering the Gettysburg Address

"FOUR SCORE AND seven years ago." Thus, begins the first of the two-hundred-and-seventy-two words of President Abraham Lincoln's less than three-minute delivery of his most well-known speech. Were there ever words more carefully weighed? In contrast to former Secretary of State Edward Everett's lengthy speech, President Lincoln's address at Gettysburg was shockingly brief. Everett, a close friend of renowned orator Daniel Webster, delivered a formal address that day that went almost two hours. Since the President would be giving only the dedication itself, those in attendance would have expected his remarks to be somewhat brief. But his words were so few that when Lincoln returned to his seat next to Everett the audience was stunned into silence, followed by only a smattering of applause. Their reaction led the President to say quietly to Everett that his address had fallen flat. (His perception has since been belied by the renown of his speech and its countless recitations.) Even our wildest guesses of how many times such recitations have been made would be far shy of the mark. This is a story of how that number was supposed to have included me.

As a sixth grader, I was thrilled to be selected from my class to recite the Gettysburg Address at a Memorial Day service at the North Springfield cemetery. Always a good student, eager to please, I memorized the speech, word by word over the weeks leading up to Memorial Day. The day I was to deliver the address, I put on my favorite blue dress with a sailor's collar that I had washed by hand and ironed. (How I loved the color of that dress and the way its white collar fell crisply over my shoulders both front and back!)

Since Dad had no choice but to paint houses on weekends as a second source of income, he couldn't drive me to the cemetery, which fell to my older brother Brian. Looking back, I can only imagine how hard it must have been for my father to miss watching his only daughter that day and, instead, to spend the day carrying a bucket of paint up and down a ladder, applying a brush to the wood siding on someone else's house, stroke after repetitive, tiring stroke. I don't remember feeling upset about it. My job that day was to deliver the Gettysburg Address, with or without my father in the audience.

At the cemetery, I stood next to Brian near the temporary stage that had been erected, more than a little nervous. Reading the printed program, I was shocked to see the name of a different girl who would deliver the Gettysburg Address. Confused, hurt and upset, I turned to my brother to announce firmly that I wanted to leave. Having practiced that speech so often that for weeks every morning, its words had been the first thing to rush into my mind, there was no way I was going to watch a different girl, one I didn't even know, take my place. When Brian, perplexed, asked me several times if I was sure I wanted to leave, I was adamant. So, he did as I asked and drove me home.

Later that afternoon, after my father arrived home in his paint-spattered shirt, pants, and work boots, with small splotches of paint on his face and hands, I told him the story. Though my chest still ached with disappointment, I managed not to cry. When he looked over the program, he noticed it was two-sided. Presumably to save costs, a single program had been printed with the schedule for the Springfield and North Springfield commemorations on opposite sides. There, on the side of the program for the North Springfield program, he pointed out my name. Seeing my mistake brought a pink flush of embarrassment to my cheeks. I pictured the moment when they called me to the stage to deliver the Gettysburg Address and, since I had insisted on leaving early, the audience was met with silence.

While pondering what lessons I could harvest from this difficult experience, slowly they came to me.

*1. Question your first assumption.*

Standing at the cemetery next to Brian, who knows what was running through my head? My mother had died less than two years earlier. Likely this trauma was still running rampant in my system, wreaking havoc with my thoughts and impressions. How I wish I (or my brother) had paid more attention and taken the time to question my assumption.

*2. Find a way to resolve or accept what happened.*

In an imaginary scene, I am eleven again. Since I have worked so hard to memorize President Lincoln's address and because of my mistake at leaving, that night my father suggests that I deliver it to him and my brothers in the living room. I stand nervously before them, but after I speak those first few famous words my voice grows stronger all the way to the end. I finish to their enthusiastic applause as I take a deep bow.

This scene reminds me of when Janelle, our younger daughter, was in middle school. Like so many young people in Ann Arbor, Michigan, for several years she spent two weeks at Camp Algonquin on Burt Lake, a four-hour drive north on U.S.-75. (Even decades later, some of these same campers still affix bumper stickers to their cars, "I would rather be at Camp Algonquin.") One summer, I'm proud to say, Janelle completed the camp's Long Swim, since discontinued for safety reasons. The Long Swim was one mile across the lake, a brief rest, and then the return trip, which to the swimmers must have seemed much longer than the first leg. Numerous campers gave up along the way, pulling their exhausted bodies into nearby boats driven by camp staff. But Janelle kept at it, stroke after stroke.

By the time she walked up on shore, completely spent, instead of the scores of cheering campers who greeted the earlier finishers, only a couple of her close friends stood there to welcome her back. Other than the staff member in the nearby boat, everyone else was long gone. Janelle was justifiably proud of her accomplishment. She had set out, with the same determination that has always been part of who she is, to complete the Long Swim. Pushing herself beyond what she thought were her limits, she persevered. She had done it.

At a banquet on the last night of camp, the camp staff handed out honors, including certificates for those who had successfully completed the swim. As each camper walked to the front of the room to receive a certificate, campers and camp staff gave a hearty cheer. Janelle waited patiently for her name to be called, but suddenly they were done and on to bestowing a different award. She was stunned, crestfallen. Later, she learned that because she had arrived so much later than the other swimmers, her name had been inadvertently left off the list of completers.

On the day after Janelle arrived home from camp and told us her sad story, we took our daughters out for dinner at a restaurant typically reserved for special occasions. Over dessert, accompanied by her older sister's gentle tabletop drumroll with an exaggerated flourish, I presented Janelle with the Long Swim certificate I had created that afternoon, printed on high quality paper. Said another way, it's never too late to receive (or give yourself) the recognition you deserve, even if you need to recreate the scenario in some way, even years after the fact. It is *never* too late.

*3. As much as the results, treasure the process.*

To this day, although I can no longer recite it from memory, I love the Gettysburg Address. Reciting the address at the cemetery that day would have been rewarding. But even without that satisfaction, to this day I savor those hours of practice through which I imprinted President Lincoln's powerful words into my mind and stamped the wisdom they imparted into the fiber of my being.

*4. Forgive yourself and others and then let go.*

As for my daughter, no one can take away her hard-fought Long Swim success (or, for that matter, finishing the one marathon she would run many years later). As for me, it was not the end of the world that no one read the Gettysburg Address that day at the North Springfield cemetery. The moment passed. People were puzzled. Then life resumed its unending flow, a perfect and ever-present example of letting go.

## *Questions to Ponder*

- Is there an unresolved disappointment in your life?
- Even if time has passed, can you think of a way you might resolve it?

## CHAPTER 5

# Make Peace (Not War) Within

"The Ultimate Dimension" is an audio recording of a meditation retreat with Thich Nhat Hanh, the much-loved Vietnamese Zen Buddhist monk who teaches meditation and mindfulness in ways that we can fit into our busy lives. One day while listening to his words, I feel the inner click of a major insight as if my mind has flipped on a switch it has been waiting a long time to find.

In the recording, Nhat Hanh talked quietly about the concept of *making war within*. After listening to his words, over the course of the day I try to watch my thoughts carefully. With this closer look, I am embarrassed to see how many of these thoughts plant seeds of conflict rather than of peace. For example, I look back on what I perceive to be wrongs against me, conjure up negative images of what the future might hold, re-run upsetting conversations (typically in a way that puts me on top), and fan the fires of negative emotions.

As I ponder this new insight, I re-run a scene that took place a few days earlier. While in a rush to meet someone, rather than wait at a traffic light I turned instead down a parallel side street that ended at a stop sign at the foot of a bridge. Despite a cluster of trees limiting my view on the bridge-side, a quick glance to my right assured me all was clear. Seeing no cars approaching on the left, I began making a right-hand turn when a sudden string of profanities pierced the air. Puzzled, I turned to see a bicyclist appear out of nowhere. Decked out in a neon bright shirt and black bike shorts, he stood astride his bike, screaming at me.

As my heart raced at the possibility that I might have hit him, through the window I apologized several times. But after he crossed in front of my car and sped away, continuing to spew profanities, my panic and regret began to morph into indignation. After all, I *did* look both ways and *he* was the one racing down the sidewalk on the wrong side of the road into a blind spot. Surely, he was not entirely free of blame. And were his loud curses necessary or even called for? The more I looked back on it, the angrier I felt. But as I found myself, over the next day, continuing to seethe, I began to wonder why in the world I was filling my mind with playbacks of this scene. Did I really want to relive it over and over, flooding myself with ever more negativity?

As I gave more thought not just to this scene but also to my general tendency to continue to feed my negative emotions, I remembered another way I "make war within": my tendency to concoct imaginary calamities in my mind, things that have never even happened (at least not yet, I tell myself). When home alone, I sometimes imagine strangers stalking the house, plotting the best way to break in. When walking alone in the woods (which, sadly, I seldom feel safe enough to do), I imagine a stranger who assaults me from behind. Driving on the highway at night, I sometimes see in my mind's eye a wildly speeding car headed straight at me toward an inevitable head-on collision. I've heard such thinking referred to as negative daydreams. Quite possibly I don't have any more negative daydreams than the average person. But because research has shown that our minds (and bodies) can exhibit as many physical signs of trauma from make-believe danger as from the real thing, I would prefer to do less of it.

As I continued to ponder, a third category of how I make mental war came up: replaying again and again moments of conflict with other people, making them grow ever larger in my mind as I obsess over how unfair or hurtful they were. For example, a member of a group I belong to says something where I take offense. Or a friend makes a joke that rankles. My husband makes an offhand comment that I transfigure into a small arrow shot to my heart. Occasionally in the middle of the night I lie in bed, eyes wide open, reliving just this kind of scenario, watching the clock until I manage, despite a haunted mind, to fall back to sleep.

In these several ways, I use my marvelous brain-mind to create or recreate bad scenes, keep alive old or imagined hurts, and conjure up negative daydreams. The teaching of Thich Nhat Hanh, though, has given me a new name for what I'm doing: *waging war within*. I wage war with other people (even if they know nothing about it) but worst of all, I wage war within, robbing only myself.

I asked myself a favorite coaching question, "What's this about?" But no easy answers came. My father tended to want to be "right." Am I still fighting against being the youngest kid and only girl, still wanting, like my Dad, to be right? In a still vivid memory from childhood, one of my older brothers complained to our father that I was washing the silverware in the soapy water with my fingers instead of using the dishcloth. After watching me for a moment, Dad said, "For goodness sakes, she can wash the silverware any way she wants to." To this day when I remember that scene, a deep satisfaction washes over me. In that moment, Dad had declared *me* to be right.

Or perhaps, after the trauma of losing my mother when I was so young, I adopted these mental habits to prepare myself mentally for future tragedies. Over the years, I've seen several therapists who have helped lead me to healthier perspectives and given me a toolbox of coping skills. One described this type of behavior with words that hit home. He called it my fear of being "chumped again."

Regardless of the reasons that might fuel this destructive habit, reframing these mental habits as *waging war within* galvanizes me to want to stop. The notion of creating war has no place in how I see myself, in my identity. Since having this insight, I have become a bit more skillful at catching myself in the act. Drawing on the wisdom of Thich Nhat Hanh, I call upon the simple but powerful habit of first taking a deep breath and then simply asking myself, gently and without judgment, "In this moment, what can I do to touch peace?"

Sometimes an answer comes. *Do a loving kindness meditation. Just let it go.* Sometimes the only answer I receive is silence, and it is enough. What's important, I believe, is that I have waved a white flag to stop the war within. Given everything we know about the human mind and psyche, I will need to repeat these steps, over and over, for the rest of my life. When I use this gentle but powerful practice, what happens to the war within? In its place, I touch the treasure I believe we all seek, perhaps more than anything else in life: instead of waging war, make peace. Be fully present not to what might be, but to what is.

## *Questions to Ponder*

- Can you think of a time when you waged war within, big or small?
- What were the circumstances?
- When this has happened, what's one tactic that has worked for you to damp down this sense of conflict?
- What's one thing you could do in such a moment to touch peace within?

CHAPTER 6

# Rein in Your Personal Rules

My husband sometimes eats crackers in the family room, rye crispbread crackers that drop a small shower of crumbs with each bite. Although I love my husband, this is one of the things he does that drives me crazy. "Please," I've asked him many times, "eat over a bowl or a plate." But despite his good intentions, he keeps forgetting, and the crumbs continue to fall.

When I'm not at home, Rick eats his crackers in peace. But when I'm there as witness, the scene unfolds something like this. As soon as he takes the first bite, I throw him *the look*. Like a kid getting caught, he gives me one of his sheepish grins that so endear him to me I can't be mad. Then he holds his hand under his chin to catch the crumbs and although I'm not entirely satisfied, I figure a win is a win and I need to take them as they come.

One day our older daughter and I were standing at the kitchen sink when I complained to her about the Rye-Cracker, Bad Guy. Turning to face me, she said matter-of-factly, "Mom, that sounds like a personal rule to me." *Is that what this is,* I asked myself? *Just a personal rule*? I sighed. (Doesn't it drive you nuts when your kids are smarter than you?)

By focusing on personal rules in this chapter, I don't mean to challenge the family and cultural norms for behavior we believe in, hold dear, and do our best to live by. Nor do I mean to criticize the appropriate expectations and boundaries parents set for their children. But ultimately, rules that qualify as personal are about personal preferences, how, in our ideal world, we want things to be.

As I try to do after experiencing an aha moment, I took a closer look at some of my behaviors, in this case to uncover more of these personal rules. Easily, I found a few more, certain there were many others on the list.

*1. The bed must be made every morning.*
In my personal rulebook, making the bed includes four steps: smooth out any slack in the sheets, straighten the blanket, shake it out over the bed, and then squarely position the quilt that serves as a bedspread (a rule made even nuttier by a sub-rule: the consumer info tag I have never cut off, despite having been disabused many years ago of my childhood fear of being arrested if I do, must be on the least visible side of the bed). I can see you rolling your eyes, and I agree. Oy vey!

*2. Curtains should be open during the day and in wild weather at least one window in each room should be open to let in fresh air.*
Since this rule also applies to the guest room, I confess that whenever we have company if by mid-morning the curtains are still closed, I watch for a chance to sneak quickly into the room to open them and, in summer, to crack open a window.

*3. Before turning in for the night, the dishes must be washed, countertops wiped clean, and any bits of kitchen scraps in the sink strainer basket knocked into the compost bin or–only if necessary–churned through the disposal.*

*4. Before being stored for the winter, screens must be vacuumed.*
Once during a wave of late spring bliss, I decided to install the screens and crank open a few windows. In the corner of the basement, I found the most heavily used screens still covered in last fall's end-of-warm-weather lint, pollen and dirt. Since the un-vacuumed state of these screens violated one of my rules, I was not happy about it. I confess, though, that while I vacuumed the screens, I found no bugs or other signs that their winter storage had done them (or us) a whit of harm. Instead, what I found staring me in the face was … yup, another personal rule.

As I mulled over this list, which was just a short list of many more such rules I could dredge up, I got what my daughter was saying. My personal rules are not handed down from on high. They are only that–my *personal* rules.

When I'm away from home, many of these rules are ignored with nothing the worse for wear.

During a good share of my twenty-six years of service as an administrator at the University of Michigan, one of my jobs was to develop and revise policies for university faculty and staff. In that work, I took great pride in incorporating into my writing a rule a mentor taught me along the way: good policy lays out in clear, easy-to-understand language *who does what*; bad policy suggests, usually written in hard-to-digest, jargon-heavy language, *something happens.*

Over the years, I came to believe well-written policy is important, especially in large, complex organizations. Even though there wasn't much glory in developing or revising formal policy, I liked to think that to this day when people read the policies I worked hard to improve, even though they may still grumble, maybe, just maybe, they do less head scratching than they would have done otherwise. They at least have a clear sense of *who does what.*

In pondering my personal rules, I wondered if, when I retired, I brought my policy-writing ways home with me. I could even picture my personal rules in a bound rulebook, sorted into categories such as *Eating*, *Daily Rituals,* and *General Order of the Home.* Not a pretty picture, if peace and harmony are my main goals, which they are (most of the time).

What's the bottom line here? In answering, let me offer you a few new rules (I know, I know—I'm hopeless):

1. Acknowledge which of your rules might be *personal rules.*
2. Soften your personal rules. Sort out legitimate consequences from personal quirks.
3. Feel free to follow your personal rules, but don't expect others to do the same.
4. Put relationships first.

Would I rather have no crumbs on my husband's chair or a peaceful evening at home? What's the harm in leaving a few dirty dishes on the kitchen counter at night? Or, if we've had dinner guests, it's late, and I'm exhausted, what's wrong with cleaning up in the morning? If a houseguest leaves the curtains closed, what's the worst that could happen? When I'm away, does it really matter whether my husband follows my rules?

I'll close with a "rule" I heard during the days of Total Quality Management as a simple, one-size-fits-all replacement for the endless volumes of written rules and regulations on organizational shelves, a rule I shared numerous times with our daughters, typically as they were about to go out for the evening: *Use your best judgment, at all times.* Is even this advice open to interpretation? Yes. And that, my friends, is the point.

## *Questions to Ponder*

- Does at least one personal rule of yours come to mind? What might you do to recognize it as such and soften your judgment of others?
- Might you be able to write a useful personal rule about lightening up your expectations about others abiding by your personal rules? (Hmm … that could be an interesting twist.)

CHAPTER 7

# Lessons from an Orchid Graveyard

LUCKILY FOR ME, one of my friends is an orchid lover. After living for almost forty years in Ann Arbor, a few years ago she moved to a different state in the Midwest after she found the perfect apartment in a retirement community near her family, one with reasonable rent and a walkout patio adjacent to a large park.

My friend was a founding member of the Sunday night dinner group that Rick and I have been members of for thirty years. Whenever she hosted our group, I walked through her front door, removed my shoes, gave her a hello hug, and then headed straight for the small room just beyond her galley kitchen. In that small space, designed for utilities, my friend had created a personal paradise filled with blooming orchids, a most welcome treat, especially during the dark months of winter.

My friend's spellbinding assortment of orchids, hung from hooks or rested on slatted trays filled with water, kept good company there with a washer and dryer, a utility sink, and a small table with an automatic drip coffeemaker perched beneath a playful collection of unique cups that hung on a lattice wall. Her collection included the ever-popular Phalaenopsis (Phal), in the Dendrobium genus (Dends for short), which are common but gloriously diverse in color and size. Also on display were orchids in the Oncidiums genus (Oncs), including one playfully named Sharry Baby. My friend's collection also included plants in the showy, large-flowered Cattleya family, including one called Jewel Box Scheherazade, named for a Persian queen. To me, being among my friend's orchids when they were in bloom was like stepping through a door into flower-lover's heaven.

Many years ago, inspired by my friend's orchids, I decided to give orchid growing a try, buying a brightly colored Phal. At the time, I knew nothing of *scale*, small, crusty, armor-like brown discs, spread by insects so small it takes a magnifying glass to see them, that form on plant leaves. Out of the blue, the leaves on my Phal were covered with a sticky, syrupy substance (ironically called honeydew), which is a sure sign of scale infestation. By the time I realized what was happening, the plant was too far gone to save. I had no choice but to admit defeat and throw it in the trash, which is agony for a plant lover like me.

While my friend was preparing for her big move, she called me one day to ask if I wanted to adopt some of her orchids. Despite my earlier failure with the Phal, I was thrilled. Although I believed she was wise to make the move while she still had plenty of time and energy to build a new community of friends, my heart was heavy as the date for her move approached. For this reason, the idea of becoming caregiver for a handful of her darling orchids, of bringing this special part of her into my house, was especially welcome.

When I arrived at my friend's house, she gave me five orchids, as well as fertilizer, orchid potting mixture, and an oversized, stainless steel bowl for annual repotting. She also demonstrated how to water the orchids weekly. "Hold them over the utility sink and give them a good drenching from the spray nozzle. Follow that up with water mixed with a healthy dose of fertilizer." Handing me several plant hangers, she added: "Hang them outside in the summer. They will love it." She then pointed out the flat plastic stick buried in the planting material next to the edge of each orchid's pot. The name of the orchid (if known), its purchase date, and the month and year of its last repotting was written in pencil on each stick. "Repot every year," she told me, "because over time the potting mixture breaks down."

After carefully loading the orchids and supplies into my car, I walked back inside to thank my friend and say goodbye. She asked me to hang on a moment and disappeared into the back room, which was now, sadly, just a utility room. When she returned, she handed me a plastic bag filled with a collection of the flat plastic sticks. “Here,” she said, handing it to me. “This is my orchid graveyard.” When I shot her a quizzical look, she explained, “These sticks are from orchids that didn’t make it. Orchids aren’t easy to grow and can be fickle. Also, you never know if you have the right environment for a certain orchid, and if you don’t, it’s not your fault. So, if one dies, don’t blame yourself. Just buy another one to take its place.”

On the drive home and during the weeks that followed, I pondered the notion of an orchid graveyard, one that I found rich in metaphor. We all have our personal “orchid graveyards”: mistakes we’ve made, dumb decisions, wrong moves, the tendency to keep doing the same thing but expecting a different result. How liberating to store such missteps in a bag of personal graveyard sticks! When something doesn’t work out, open the bag, add a marker, and then go out and try something different. We all can keep an “orchid graveyard” in the drawer.

A few years have passed and I’ve added only one plant marker to the orchid graveyard. Not bad, I figure. More importantly, I’ve added a bunch of markers to my metaphorical graveyard, and in each case, simply looked ahead to my next move.

## *Bonus lesson from my adopted orchids*

In a home that was already too full of houseplants, I had to make space for the orchids. I ended up creating a spot in the front room with a southeast exposure, some direct sunlight but not so much as to overheat or cause harm. In the first year of my role as adoptive mother to my friend’s orchids, one Phal opened its blooms to reveal a subtle blend of muted colors: pale yellow, a hint of light green, a bit of pale red, and some orange in the center. As a lover of brilliant, jewel colors, I was disappointed. In response, I simply left the Phal sitting in the front room, which we seldom used, watering it weekly but otherwise ignoring it.

But a year later, when it bloomed for a second time, something inside urged me to move it into the kitchen onto the wooden shelf on top of the partition that separated our kitchen from the family room. There, at just about at eye level, the orchid blooms frequently drew my eyes to them. During the weeks while the Phal was in bloom that year, my previous disappointment disappeared as I gradually fell in love with its muted mix of colors. Silly me, I realized, for wanting it to be more brilliant, to be something it wasn't. Beginning that year, I enjoyed its blooms thoroughly and wouldn't have changed a thing about it.

So, in addition to giving yourself the gift of an "orchid graveyard," when your "orchids" bloom, however they exist symbolically in your life, put them somewhere where you can see them often, appreciate them fully *for what they are* and savor away.

## *Questions to Ponder*

- In one or more aspects of your life, how might you give yourself permission to have and even celebrate an "orchid graveyard?"
- Thinking back to a time when you felt like you had failed, if you were to write on an "orchid stick" what you learned from the experience, what would it be?

11

# Oh, the Choices We Make

We have all a better guide in ourselves, if we would attend to it, than any other person can be.

–Jane Austen

## CHAPTER 8

# Beware Being a Search Engine Junkie

SEARCH ENGINES LIKE Google seduce us without mercy. We know this and succumb to them anyway. An important question we should ask is, "Just because I *can* look it up online, will I?"

It's true we are problem-solving creatures who love answers–the quicker, the better. When even the most trivial question bubbles up in our ever-churning minds or during conversation, more and more of us reach habitually (I would add, mindlessly) for a smartphone or computer. Finding answers this easily is like being rewarded with a delicious piece of chocolate when we press the correct lever. (What we're really after are hits of dopamine, a neurotransmitter that plays a key role in the brain's centers for pleasure and reward. But that's a complicated conversation I'll leave to the scientists.) Cha-ching!

It's not uncommon these days on dining room tables for a laptop, tablet or smartphone to be within easy reach, as if setting a place for a skin-and-bones kid with one humongous brain. I confess at times I need to stop myself from doing this. And toward the end of a meal, even though we're not quite finished, I've been known to give in to temptation, typing some topic into the search window on our tablet.

How spoiled we are by this speed and convenience! Even the short time it takes to leave (or retrieve) a voicemail message has become intolerably long. Since I can no longer assume that family members or friends who call the house will leave a voicemail message, I've trained myself to check caller ID after being away from the house. One of our daughters no longer has the patience to spend the thirty seconds it takes for her call to enter voicemail land, listen for the umpteenth time to voicemail instructions, and then, most annoying of all, be forced to wait for the beep. I confess that although I *do* wait for the beep to leave a message, in those few seconds my foot taps impatiently as if it has a will of its own.

One night at a dinner in our home, one of our friends paused from eating chicken thighs baked with sun-dried tomatoes and sautéed green beans mixed with roasted tomatoes and slivered almonds, to pull out his smartphone. I can't recall the question that had grabbed his attention. A good five minutes later, though, he was still at it, the food growing cold on his plate.

I put my hand on his arm and said, "You don't have to keep looking. It's not that important." (In that moment, I imagine a time in the future when small groups of family members or friends will hold interventions for web-searching junkies diving fast down the virtual rabbit hole.) He quipped that searching was like roaming happily through row upon row of stacks in a library basement. I paused to ask, "But do you *want* to be in the stacks right now?" He smiled, put his phone away (no intervention necessary), and picked up his fork.

## *Questions to Ponder*

- Do *you* want to be "in the stacks" right now?
- How long do you want to stay?
- What else could you be doing?
- Is the question you want to answer really that important?
- What do you want? Really want?

CHAPTER 9

# Dress Up in Some Way Every Day

ONE DAY WHEN I arrived at my friend Barb's house, she called down to me from upstairs to make myself at home, that she would be down shortly. A few minutes later, from my comfortable spot on her living room sofa I watched her walk slowly down the stairs. That day, she was wearing a blouse with a lacey layer on top of a soft jersey-like cloth beneath, along with a matching skirt sewn of a heavier cloth that echoed the same woven design. Her entire outfit was a rich periwinkle, one of my favorites, with its blend of blue and purple, a laudable mix of function and beauty. Finding her clothing, and my friend, lovely to look at, I took a few minutes to study the cloth and then, because she is a close friend, to feel its smooth, pleasing texture between my fingers.

This admiration, this close look at what my friend was wearing, happens almost every time I see her. (I must add, though, that my friend's lovely clothes pale in comparison to how she dresses herself *within,* which is ultimately what makes me so glad to be in her company. Despite having faced, with a great deal of aplomb and courage, a long line of serious health challenges, Barb greets people with a smile and is generous with her time and energy. In our friendship, simply being with her is by far the highlight of whatever we do.) That day, seated on my friend's sofa, I cleared my throat after taking a sip of steaming green tea on the small table in front of me, sat up straight, and then, while gesturing formally at her, offered up a pronouncement, "You, my friend, are a woman who brings elegance to the world."

She smiled her thanks and then told me a story. For more than thirty years, my friend's many health challenges came at her in a dark parade that would leave most people in a puddle of despair. Yet through it all she continued to dig deep and persevere. On a day years ago, she told me, she'd begun to wonder how much longer she had to live. That very day, she explained, she made a pact with herself to "dress up" every day for the rest of her life.

As she talked, the reason why she dresses so nicely came clear. Like lots of people, I dress up only for special occasions like weddings, bar or bat mitzvahs, receptions. My friend, though, dresses up every single day. Knowing how much I enjoy her beautiful clothing, I pondered the positive effect she must also have on the other people in her life. By dressing up, I expect she makes *herself* feel good. Plus, many of the people she sees throughout her day must appreciate the beauty of her clothes in much the same way I do. By dressing up she also makes *other people* feel good. As my thoughts shifted to my own clothing, I began to wonder whether there were ways I could be more like my friend … and still be myself.

Throughout a long career at a university, I enjoyed owning and wearing a career wardrobe. Faithfully following such trends as "dress for success," "color yourself beautiful," and "mix and match," over the years I purchased a collection of short jackets in a mix of colors and textures, tending toward the jewel tones I'm known for wearing. (A former colleague still teases me when we run into each other, which we often do early on Saturday at the local farmer's market, for how often I'm wearing something purple). I also kept my collection of silk and woven scarves and a set of decorative pins I purchased over the years or that were given to me. Then there's my handmade wooden jewelry box with its four drawers of earrings I've purchased over the years, a collection I continue to build by buying a new pair three or four times a year. Looking back on my career years, I recalled how much I enjoyed selecting some of these items as I assembled an outfit each morning. I also remembered how good it felt to leave the house feeling a bit dressed up, and, based on the compliments I sometimes received from co-workers, to add, in some small way, to the aesthetics of where I worked.

Since retiring from the university in the summer of 2011 to focus on my coaching career and a host of other interests, the clothing I enjoyed wearing as a professional had spent most of its time in dark closets or folded neatly in drawers. What did I wear instead? At best, my choice of clothes at that time was what I would call pedestrian. Most mornings I chose a knit shirt from one of two stacks, short and long sleeves to match the season, and a pair of jeans. In winter months, I then pulled on a finely woven, black wool sweater that had practically become my signature (the day I eventually threw it away, after it developed a few very visible holes, was a sad one), or a solid color sweater or fleece top. If I had been asked to put a name to my post-career style of dressing, I would have said *comfortable.*

There were, however, practical reasons for how plainly I dressed. Since I am at home much of the time and because my husband and I, to conserve energy, keep the house on the cool side during the winter and use air conditioning only on blisteringly hot days in the summer, I dress first and foremost for the weather. On cold winter days, I pull on the same pair of baggy flannel-lined jeans I've been wearing for so long (hand-me-downs from one of my daughters) that the red flannel at the crease of where I roll up the leg bottoms is badly frayed. When I picture the "union suits" my grandfather wore between the first true winter day until well past spring thaw, it brings a smile to my face and makes me wonder if part of me is carrying on the tradition. Still pondering my friend's habit of dressing up, I asked myself how I had slid into such strictly practical, unaesthetic ways of dressing.

Perhaps, I thought, I was still, after more than fifty years, rebelling against my stepmother's decision, shortly after she married my father, to put herself in charge of how I dressed, as evidenced by the pile of clothes she laid out on my bed after she and my father returned from a shopping trip to the metropolis of Manchester, New Hampshire. Seen through my vulnerable adolescent eyes, that terrible pile in front of me, most of which I refused to wear, made me feel like I has been beaten up. (But in view of my promise to stop telling stories about her, that's all I'll say about it.) As soon as I was old enough, I found a part-time job that gave me the money, and, more importantly, the freedom to buy my own clothes.

Another value at play for me, I thought, was authenticity. But taken to an extreme, this viewpoint can lead to the notion that dressing up is somehow phony, which is not true of my friend or other people I know who dress more fashionably than I do. Suddenly I saw that the labels I used to describe my style of dress, words like *comfortable*, *authentic* and *practical*, could just as easily translate into terms like *dull*, *drab* or *boring*. In this train of thought, I found myself wondering what affect my daily choice of what to wear might be having on my mood, my frame of mind, my confidence, and even my sense of self.

With these thoughts, my mind returned to my friend, and to other friends who dress more attractively than I do, for example when going out for dinner. I decided then and there it was time for me to revisit my ways, to free myself from the set of rather boring guidelines that held sway over what I chose to wear.

A *New Yorker* cartoon by Michael Maslin shows two people conversing at some type of gathering. One of them (a quirkily dressed woman) says to her companion, "I don't have anything to say; my clothes say it all." This notion is absurd, of course, which is why it's funny. As I mentioned, how we dress *within* (and what we say) is even more important than the clothes we choose to dress in. But then I ask myself, "Why not both?" In answering that question, I made a commitment to begin each day by consciously and mindfully choosing my inner attire—my attitude, my outlook, my mood, my perspective.

As for the outer me, I decided it was time for me to take a lesson from my friend. I didn't then, nor would I ever have, the marvelous collection of clothes Barb has purchased over the years. But at the same time, I decided, I could and would make some changes.

For one, I moved my collection of scarves to make them more accessible. I also placed my collection of pins in a more convenient spot. (Wearing pins may be passé, but who cares?) Next, I identified which of the jackets that I wore as a professional I could comfortably wear in my new life, and then I hung them in a more visible part of my closet as a reminder. Since drafting this chapter, I have also given away a stack of my more boring fleece tops, and to take their place have purchased (and wear) more print sweaters and print knit shirts in place of solids. Having added clothing to my wardrobe that is both more alluring and more fun, even on stay-at-home days, I now try to dress up a bit more, if only in small ways such as choosing a pair of earrings I especially love.

This thought process reminded me of a childhood friend whose parents, when they took her shopping for some new clothes, believed the clothes should stay in the drawer until my friend truly needed them. My guess is that in a similar vein, a lot of us "save" some of our loveliest clothing for special occasions. I invite everyone to treat every day in some small way as a special occasion, like my friend Barb. Let's not save our beautiful things. Let's *wear* them as a gift both to ourselves and to the people we see. Let's follow the admirable lead of my friend and each, in our own way, dress up every day.

## *Questions to Ponder*

- With respect to the clothing you wear, what's one thing you could do to enjoy your beautiful things more often, and share them with the world?
- As for your *inner* self, how do you tend to dress yourself for the day? This morning, for example, what kind of *attitude* did you put on?
- What one *way of being* is hanging in your inner closet that you would prefer to move to the attic?
- What's one thing you could do to dress more beautifully within?

CHAPTER 10

# Expect Change (Especially When You Least Expect It)

As I WRITE the first draft of this chapter, my husband and I have been living in Michigan for what I call the longest rest stop in history. When we arrived in 1985, we planned to stay for only the two years it would take Rick to earn his master's degree in architecture. So far, the "rest stop" has stretched into almost thirty years–long enough to own a home for most of that time, raise our two daughters and then watch from a distance as they created interesting lives (one in San Francisco and the other in Brooklyn, New York), and long enough to discover and enjoy many outdoor and cultural treasures in Ann Arbor, the state of Michigan (including the Upper Peninsula), and some of the gems in nearby Ontario, Canada.

But during all this time, our deep desire to move back to the Green Mountains continued to burn brightly no matter how many years passed. This was true for three main reasons.

*1. Vermont plays an important part in our history, individually and as a couple.* Vermont is my home state, and it's also where my husband and I met, fell in love, and married. The magnetic pull of this beautiful state, where our love and partnership grew, has only strengthened, over time, our resolve to return someday.

*2. Members of our immediate and extended families, as well as many close friends, live in Vermont or within a day's travel.*

- Our younger daughter, a professional musician and designer, has made New York City her home, renting a light-filled apartment in

Brooklyn. If we were to move back to Vermont, what a treat it would be to shrink the distance between us to an easy day's drive (with the welcome alternative of hopping aboard a train).

- My brother Peter and his wonderful wife Martha live in culture-rich Burlington, Vermont.
- On Rick's side of the family, a cousin's daughter and her larger-than-life husband (in the same generation as our daughters) have settled in nearby Montpelier (a town squarely in our sights as we pondered a possible return).
- Other family members on both sides—a brother, aunts and an uncle, nieces and a nephew, cousins, and a bunch of kids two generations behind us–live in or near New York City (where my husband grew up), as well as outside Boston and in tiny Rhode Island. All of them would be an easy drive away.
- In parts of Vermont both north and south, long-term friendships (many of them reaching back to when we were in our early twenties) also beckon us home.

*3. We thrive on the outdoor activities Vermont offers year-round.*
Hiking, canoeing, kayaking, cross-country skiing–we love it all, and in every season (well, okay, maybe not mud season), holding firm to the belief there's no such thing as bad weather, only bad choice in clothing.

In response to this powerful inner urge, in 2010 my husband and I made what we claimed at the time to be a firm decision to move back to Vermont after he retired. How my heart soared! Then, late in 2011, a monkey wrench plunked down into the gears of our plan. While in San Francisco walking with our daughter on a path in the woods near her home, I was stunned to hear her say that she and our son-in-law, also an Ann Arbor townie, had been mulling over a move back to Ann Arbor.

If they decided to have a family, she said (enunciating the word *if* like a bell warning me not to get my hopes too high), they would not want to raise a child in the city. Also, she said, they wanted to buy a home, but not in an earthquake zone, where desperate want-to-be homebuyers bid on homes and lay down earnest money like "crazies." (This term came to me from a close friend during the time she and her husband, along with their daughter and son-in-law, were in the market to buy a home in the Bay area. Then they found a house on a high point overlooking the Huckleberry Botanic Regional Preserve, where the uplift and folding of land over eons has carved a series of ridges where light and shadow, regardless of the weather, paint ever-changing patterns throughout the day as the sun moves across the sky. By turns verdant green and dry, the view is stunning year-round. Upon stepping down onto their deck for the first time, I was rooted in place, speechless at the grandeur before me and awed by their incredible good fortune. So, for a heap of excellent reasons my friends, and their daughter and her husband, in purchasing this gorgeous home, joined the ranks of the "crazies.")

After hearing the news from our daughter that she and Ben might be moving back to Ann Arbor, and before talking with my husband, I had a conversation with myself. *Of course, a move back to Michigan makes perfect sense for the kids. It's their home. They love it here. Good job opportunities. A liberal, culturally rich city where two professional incomes can buy a nice home. Plus, they would enjoy all the perks of having family nearby, including, if they decided to have a child someday, backup childcare only a phone call away and time away from the kids when they need it. (Our son-in-law's parents also live in Ann Arbor, along with their daughter and her family. So, for them, having Brenna and Ben return to Ann Arbor would mean having their entire immediate family in the same town—a situation almost unheard of these days, at least among my boomer friends.)* During this inner dialogue with myself, a far-fetched dream began to feel possible, even real. How I have envied friends whose grandkids live nearby, especially when their grandkids are just a drive across town. The possibility, even probability, that I could become one of them flooded me with happiness.

But in the same moment, my heart sank. What of our long-standing plans to move home to Vermont? What would we do? How could we ever choose? For the time being, Rick and I decided to put our plans on hold, not to jump to any conclusions, and certainly not make any decisions, but simply to wait and see.

Less than a year after our daughter's announcement, the story took another, more momentous turn. One night the kids called us on FaceTime. With the two of them standing next to each other, our son-in-law announced that our daughter was pregnant. [Up to that moment, our daughter had firmly steered us clear of expectations about whether they would have children. Later she confessed it was to keep my "grandmother hormones" in check. It turned out from the start of their romantic relationship they knew they wanted to have at least one child. They needn't have worried, though. I only ever wanted what was right for *them*.] On hearing the news, my husband and I were jubilant. When this book goes to print, our grandson will be more than four years old. (Like all books, this one has taken far longer to finish than I ever expected.)

With this new revelation of the much-anticipated birth of a grandchild, our initially ironclad plan to return to Vermont began to soften. Perhaps we could buy a small condo in Ann Arbor and have homes in both Michigan and Vermont. A post–World War II neighborhood of attached housing (now condos) in the southeast corner of the city, built around large green spaces, might be just the ticket. But a month or so after I put this idea on the table one night, my husband blurted, "I won't own two homes." And even though it hurt to admit it, I came to see that he was right.

One morning on an early walk in the winter with Rick, I showered him with questions about moving back to Vermont and what our plan might be when he retired. Suddenly the truth hit me like a two-by-four. Vermont was where we belong. Vermont was *home*. Although painfully torn, in that moment I laid claim to our long-standing dream in all its fullness—this plan to be home again among Vermont's lakes, rivers, and hiking trails; to be close to family and friends; and to face the fact that even after almost thirty years, we would never be true Michiganders.

During our daughter's pregnancy, I sank achingly into a state of envy over the luck that had fallen to our son-in-law's parents. Because we had decided we couldn't have it both ways, I forced myself to loosen my grip on the idea of being able to drive across town to see our grandchild, despite the painful knowledge that he or she would spend so much more time with their other grandparents. But echoing the Tallulah Bankhead quote next to my picture in the high school yearbook: "No one can be just like me; sometimes even I have a hard time doing it," I insisted this truth would also apply to me as a grandmother. Following in the footsteps of my own grandparents, on longer visits we would make up for the lack of living nearby. I imagined in detail the luxury of such visits, both in

Ann Arbor and, later, when our grandchild was old enough, parent-free trips to be with us in Vermont. What great fun we would have, I convinced myself.

Would it be easy to leave? Far from it. Nevertheless, did it feel like the right thing for my husband and me to do? Absolutely. Would it require sacrifice? Oh, yes. What, then, tipped the scales toward Vermont? I sat with this question for a long time until a clear, if rough-edged answer arrived. In the end, there was only one possible answer to the almost thirty-year call that ran deeper than water, this call to the spirit that would not be silenced until we finally ended this long rest stop, until we packed our things and headed east. *Vermont*, I said to myself, *we're coming home.*

*Postscript. (1)*

In this postscript and the one following, I share the true lesson of this chapter; how important it is to make plans and then be ready let go if necessary. Our older daughter, son-in-law, and grandson now own a home and live in Ann Arbor. They say they are here to stay. Our daughter is in her third and final year in a master's degree program (since completed) that will allow her to achieve her dream of being a nurse practitioner.

The firm decision I claimed to have chiseled in stone on that winter morning walk has been tempered. It began to weaken when, on my several visits to be with our new grandson, each time I flew back to Michigan I wept as the plane lifted off the ground. Then, only a few weeks after our daughter and son-in-law arrived back in Ann Arbor, Rick lightened my heart considerably when he, not I, was the one to speak what we both knew to be true: "You know those conversations we've had about moving back to Vermont? I see now just how much they were in the abstract. Now that the kids are here, it's hard to imagine leaving."

Will we eventually buy a place in Vermont? This time I'm smart enough to say only this: "Let's wait and see." All our reasons for wanting to be in Vermont are as true as ever, especially being closer to our younger daughter some of the time. My current dream is for us to buy a piece of land and build a small home or cabin my husband designs. If we do end up with two homes, the one in Vermont will be "second home," at least during our grandson's early years. Maybe over time, as he gets less interested in family and more interested in friends, the scales may shift.

The only thing I know for sure is that we don't know where this story of the pull between Michigan and Vermont will lead us. I've even started to see myself as a Vermont-Michigan woman. The lesson, it seems, is this: *sketch out a storyline for your life, sit back, and watch it change.*

*Postscript. (2)*

My advice to myself to wait and see has delivered a double dose of wisdom. As I edit this chapter a few years after drafting it, I'm here to tell you that a few months ago our younger daughter decided, for all the right reasons, that ten years in New York City was enough, that she was ready to move home to Ann Arbor. She's living with us temporarily and hoping to buy a condo. (Now a reality.) With this change, which I never dared to dream about (truly wanting only what was best for her) I have become even more a member of the envied class rather than the envious. What's happened to our plan to move back to Vermont? It has morphed into a strong intention to visit often so we can enjoy the outdoor activities we love and stay in close touch with family and friends. Now that my husband and I are both done with our careers, there is indeed much more space in our lives. How often will we visit Vermont? Since I've learned my lesson, my only answer is this: *we shall just have to wait and see.*

## *Questions to Ponder*

- As you read my story, did it remind you of any decisions you've made in life?
- Have you made what felt like a firm decision at the time only to watch it change?
- How might you apply the lessons imbedded in this chapter to your own life?

CHAPTER 11

# Go to Your High School Reunions

I WRITE THIS chapter a few days after returning from my forty-five-year high school reunion in my hometown. In 1968, we were a graduating class of 226, a number that would have been one more if, during our senior year, we hadn't lost Diana McCoy to leukemia. A full-page photo of her heart-shaped face forever smiles at us from the memoriam page in the front of our last yearbook. This reminder of her death–shortly before she was supposed to be rushing along with the rest of us into a time of life so full of promise and possibility–stood in stark contrast to our class's cheeky choice of printing almost the entire yearbook in only lowercase type to copycat the style of E. E. Cummings.

Many people graduate from high school and never look back. But the Springfield Class of 1968 has held a reunion every five years since graduation, thanks in large part to our much-loved classmate Mary Mac, a cheerleader in high school who is still urging us on all these years later. Although only the direst of circumstances could keep me away from a reunion now, it took me twenty years to decide to attend my first one. So, why did it take me so long?

Looking back at nearly every stage of my life, I see myself at the core as a happy, fun-loving person who made friends easily. But despite having good friends, my high school years will stick forever in my mind as a time of feeling self-conscious, unattractive, and, at some deep level, unloved. When, as a senior, I was chosen to be one of the girls in the local Apple Blossom Cotillion, an event "for the pretty girls" that involved dancing in floor-length gowns with a boy, I'm sure a lot of people were surprised. Heck, *I* was surprised. As to how I was possibly chosen, maybe some part of me shone through in the personal interview, which I remember enjoying. But I also seriously entertained the thought that the selection committee that year decided to choose a token "plain girl," and I fit the bill perfectly. Even worse, when I had no luck on my own finding a boy to escort me, my father called a friend of his to ask him to twist his son's arm. How humiliating!

So, to be honest with you, I waited until I felt a whole lot better about myself before driving from Michigan to Vermont to attend my first reunion. By then, I was married to the same man I still happily wake up next to every morning. At that time, we had two kids, nine and five years old, and I had a good job at a prestigious university. As a runner, I was also in good shape physically, plus I had long ago switched to wearing contact lenses, a far cry from the ugly brown-framed glasses most of us wore in those days. I had also traded in my years of long, lifeless, straight hair from high school days for a more fashionable and attractive hairstyle. Finally, in the previous year we had bought a home in a neighborhood filled with thirty-foot maple trees that we savored walking beneath in the fall when their leaves turned brilliant orange and red. In short, I felt great physically and I felt good about my life, a life I was finally willing to show my classmates.

A few minutes after I entered the Elks Club, where our reunion banquet was being held, as I waited at the bar to order a glass of wine, I re-introduced myself to one of my classmates who had always been popular in high school. "Wow!" he said, his mouth falling open, "You look really good!" I confess his words were music to my ears. It soon became clear I wasn't the only person whose reasonably good looks had been liberated only after switching to contact lenses, paying for braces to straighten crooked teeth, or, most important, waking up and embracing the best parts of ourselves.

But over the course of the weekend, I became increasingly embarrassed about how shortsighted and foolish it had been of me to wait the twenty long years it took to achieve a socially acceptable set of external circumstances before I was willing to show my face again. What I discovered at that reunion and other reunions since is that the trappings of a "good life" are most assuredly *not* what these reunions are all about. It's not about how much money we make, or how much we weigh, or how much of our hair is gray (or for the guys, how much hair they still have). It's not about whether we own a home or, if we do, how big it is. It's not about whether we ever had kids or, if we did, how they "turned out" (which makes raising kids sound like we turn them on a lathe). No, it's not about any of these things.

Instead, it's about being with people you sat next to on the bench in the elementary school black-and-white, eight-inch by ten-inch class photographs that fill a board where we got together on Saturday night to talk, laugh, eat, and dance. It's about not caring how much your friends weigh or how they look but giving them a bear hug. It's about hearing stories about yourself that long ago disappeared from your own memory bank and that you're tinkled pink to get back again, even if you refuse adamantly to believe you ever did *that.*

It's about discovering we all have unique strengths, that we have all done our share of good things and stupid things, that we have all done the best we could do every step along the way, and that we all have regrets and accomplishments, big and small. It's about seeing the first person you ever kissed or did other things with (or wish you had) that your parents would have killed you for at the time if they had only known. It's about seeing that a friend's smile never changes and nothing could make you happier than to see it and to feel it. It's about laughing out loud over all the foolish things we had done back then. It's about pausing to remember with an ache in our hearts those who are no longer here and counting ourselves among the lucky ones who still get to enjoy, at least for today, our glorious lives.

It's about hugging people who have recently lost a parent or, heaven forbid, a child, and about listening intently with aching hearts to the stories of classmates who have cancer, a bad heart, or some other major health threat and who, both of you know, although the thought remains carefully unspoken, may not be here in another five years to attend the next reunion.

It's about falling into conversations about our lives back then and learning that things weren't always as they seemed, that the appearance of a perfectly fine outer life can be a screen that hides a great deal of pain. It's about soaking up smiles and looking openly into eyes, those windows to the soul that never change and that mark the true treasure of friendship. It's about finally understanding that our life journeys are far more alike than different and that this has always been true.

It's also about connecting in deep, surprising ways with people whose names you knew but not much more. As you listen to their life stories and wisdom, your eyes open to how judgmental, closed, and blind so many of us were back then, at how little we knew about the vagaries of life. It's facing head-on the mean spiritedness that we sometimes threw at each like darts back then, and pausing to forgive each other and ourselves for doing it.

In the end, it's about walking away feeling filled up and grateful that you were a part of that baby boomer graduating class, one of that unique group of young men and women who continue to weave their way into your life every five years but who, in truth, walk with you every day. Do our cups runneth over? Indeed, they do.

So, if you're one of those people who have sworn an oath to avoid reunions, I urge you to think again. I have heard story after story from people who dragged themselves reluctantly to reunions, holding in their minds the very lowest of expectations of what they would find. But by the time the reunion was over, they walked away practically glowing, richly rewarded, deeply grateful they went. There are no guarantees, of course, but for most of us the older we get the smarter we are about what's truly important. When you attend a reunion, the eyes that look upon you when you walk in the door are very different eyes from those many years ago. The chance to see yourself through those softer, wiser eyes just may be one of the greatest gifts you ever receive.

## *Questions to Ponder*

- In what ways have you grown since high school? What changes have there been in the eyes you see the world with?
- What parts of yourself are you most proud of?
- If you have steered clear of reunions, what has held you back?

- Are there circumstances or hurts from younger years that you would do yourself a favor to forgive?
- Among the people you care deeply for, what are the types of "flaws" you don't even notice or that you put squarely in the backseat?
- Over time, what's one way you have become more able to focus on what's truly important?

## CHAPTER 12

# Sometimes (Sigh) Good Fences Do Make Good Neighbors

After twenty-seven years in our home an epiphany came to me, one that gave me the blessing to do something, in my heart, I did not want to do.

We live on the northeast side of Ann Arbor, a richly diverse neighborhood that's home to modest as well as stately houses (some of them historic); softball fields that second as soccer fields for kids on Saturday mornings; a neighborhood park whose large sandbox is full of trucks, plastic pails and shovels, and other donated toys; lots of towering maple trees; an elementary school that has been transformed into a kindergarten through eighth-grade STEAM school (Science, Technology, Engineering, Arts, and Math) with a long wait list; a public bus route; a community center; an African American church; and, only a short walk away, walking paths and a park on the Huron River, including the Cascades, a series of descending pools leading to a canoe portage, a place so wildly popular in the summer that despite the city park's addition of multiple parking options there remains an overflow. As a bonus, in only twenty-five minutes we can walk to the university or downtown.

Another important part of being mostly delighted about where we live is having good neighbors. Our neighbor to the south is a lovely woman who sets the standard for staying active and fit into old age. Unlike most people her age, she still shovels her own driveway unless the snow is exceptionally heavy. She's a role model for how to age gracefully. Our neighbors across the street are flower gardeners extraordinaire, whose gardens have been featured in the city's annual garden tour not once but twice. Plus, in the winter, they hang more than three hundred and fifty Christmas bulbs from four ornamental trees on the street side of their house. The many-colored globes sparkle in the sun and dance lightly in the wind, a vision straight out of a fairyland.

There are, though, two downsides to where we live. The main one is we live on a busy street, something I gave not a single thought to on the day a realtor showed me the house in 1987, where, within the hour, I had signed an earnest agreement before my architect husband even set eyes on the place (upon seeing the house, he endorsed my recommendation). But traffic noise isn't the focus of this chapter.

The other big downside to where we live is the house to our north. In the first few years after we bought the house and moved in, a married couple lived there who would sometimes host jam sessions, with drumming that went far into the night (the kind of gathering I might have enjoyed if we hadn't had two young kids and jobs to get to early the next morning). Then they turned the place into a rental, with a string of tenants who were lousy neighbors. Several renters in a row left barking dogs alone in the backyard for long stretches of time. (We began to wonder if owning a barking dog was a rental requirement.) Another couple had what seemed to be knock-down, drag-out fights in the middle of the night with much screaming.

After the couple that owned the house divorced, one of them moved in, beginning a string of good years, or at least peaceful ones. But while we appreciated the greater quiet, the backyard remained an issue. Largely neglected, it had gone progressively downhill over the years, especially along the back of the lot, where, to keep the wires clear, every few years the electric company uses chainsaws to cut back the trees and shrubs growing along the fence, which, when they're done, looks like a bad haircut.

One person who lived there for a time (with the owner) with whom I became friendly, mentioned something about the house going into foreclosure, after which my husband and I fantasized about buying the place and either renovating it or tearing it down. Then once more, the owner moved out and rented the place, this time to a friendly enough guy (while waiting at the bus stop he smiled a lot and flashed the peace sign at passersby) who, unfortunately, tended to hoard.

During the two years he lived there, the piles of stuff grew, including haphazard stacks under the breezeway in front of the house that became tall, scary piles favored by a local skunk. Just inside the cyclone fence, two used kid car seats sat, uncovered, on the ground, slowly becoming usable only as homes for mice and other rodents. Along the back of the house leaned a stack of worn-out realtor signs. A canoe sat face up to the rain, home to generations of mosquitoes. Except for the narrow strip of land next to the street, which the tenant kept cut back to legal height to avoid receiving a ticket from the city, plants and trees in the yard next door grew (or died) unattended. Also, hundreds of Norway maple saplings from a few inches tall up to ten feet or more had taken root, and the tall spruce tree in the backyard, its branches more naked each year, was all but dead.

So, what's the epiphany that came to me? For many years, I'd waited and held out hope that the situation next door would improve. But on the morning when I wrote this chapter, the last of my hope drained away like the final, slow drops of a dying stream. I didn't want to place blame. Like everyone alive, the person renting the house had both joys and problems. "Doing the best one can" was a force almost certainly at work here. We all have personal challenges and demons. Plus, despite being a strong believer in the power of choice and taking responsibility for our lives, I know hard times fall on people due to biases and prejudice galore, ever-widening economic inequity, and, at times, plain old bad luck. Although it's true my husband and I have worked hard and done our best to make good decisions, good luck and the privilege of race and class have also helped to smooth our way.

A few years after we moved into our home, Rick designed and built a thirty-foot-long cedar privacy fence to hide some of the house next door so we could better enjoy our time on the deck, which we used almost every day in the summer. Looking hard at this very fence is what sparked my epiphany. I've always been of the mind to agree with the Robert Frost line, "*Something there is that doesn't love a wall.*" (As a native Vermonter, I grew up with the well-known verses of this famous New England poet). But sadly, the privacy fence was not enough. As my husband and I looked ahead to selling our home, with visions of finding a quieter place to live and land enough for a larger garden, fruit trees, and berry bushes, as I wrote these words I gave myself—I gave us–permission to build a wall, to be like the misguided neighbor in Frost's poem who refuses to budge an inch from his rigid belief that *good fences make good neighbors.*

I pictured building a tall wooden fence along most of the property line that would give us, and the people who would own our home after us, privacy from the sad, unsightly state of things next door. As we poured concrete around each post, I would whisper an apology to Mr. Frost in the hope that he would understand. It's wise to be patient and to believe that things can get better. But sometimes, despite some regret, it's best to do what we believe must be done.

*Postscript.* Thankfully, the most recent renter next door moved out after filling two large dumpsters with trash and moving his remaining possessions in multiple trips with a rental van. (Where he had stored all his belongings at the house will remain a mystery.) When the owner moved back in, it was a good day. So, no fence—yet. Nevertheless, the lesson stands: for peace of mind it's not only okay but even important sometimes to take actions we would, in some ways, rather not take at all.

## *Questions to Ponder*

- Has there been a time in your life when, for good reasons, you chose a less than ideal course of action?
- What did you learn from that situation?
- Is there any action now in your life that you're being called to take even though you're on the fence about it (pun intended)?
- What would it be like to forgive yourself sometimes for not always being to take what feels like the best path?

CHAPTER 13

# Turn Off the TV

IN 1983, MY father and stepmother flew from their home in New Hampshire to Iowa to meet our younger daughter, who was less than two weeks old. Before having heart bypass surgery, which took place a few days after they returned home, Dad insisted on making this trip to hold this grandchild in his arms, his seventh and almost certainly his last.

At dinner one night during their visit, in a spirit of innocent curiosity our four-year-old daughter turned to my stepmother to ask, "Is it true that when you get home, you turn the TV on before you take off your coat?" Quizzical, my stepmother turned to look straight at me. A deep blush colored my cheeks. In response to my stepmother's look, the best I could muster was a shrug and a short reply, "What can I say? You know I can't stand television." My daughter was simply repeating a story she had heard me tell too many times, which leads me back in time to my earliest memories of watching television.

As a kid, I watched some television, but back in the 1950s there was far less television to watch. My brother Peter and I could watch cartoons and westerns on Saturday mornings, and at night we watched such family favorites as *Father Knows Best, The Adventures of Ozzie and Harriet*, and *Leave It to Beaver* (whose characters included our "relative" Eddie Haskell). But beginning in my teens and into my twenties, I became increasingly critical of television and its effects on people (including me).

In high school, on days when I came straight home from school, I relished the sweet quiet of the empty television screen that gave off nothing more than a dim reflection of what sat in front of it. (For the moment, we'll ignore my off-and-on habit of watching the soap opera *General Hospital.)* The peaceful spell, though, would be broken as soon as my stepmother walked into the house at the end of each workday. Yes, even before taking off her coat, she would switch on the television.

To me, a blaring TV in the room with no one watching it feels like having an unkempt, long-lost relative show up at the door, barge in uninvited, and plunk down into an easy chair, where he munches loudly on the snacks he rudely helped himself to, spewing crumbs onto his lap, the chair and the carpet near his feet; just the type of visitor one wants to show quickly to the door, pointing "out" with a finger.

Due to this early aversion, I watched almost no television well into my twenties. One time when I still smoked cigarettes (thank heavens, not for long), I was seated around a table at a restaurant with friends when I turned to ask a man seated at the table next to us for a match to light my cigarette. He pulled out a lighter with a flourish, smiled, and said, "Flick a Bic!" Puzzled, I asked, "What did you say?" After he repeated himself and I gave him another confused look, he shrugged, helped me light my cigarette, and turned back to his companions. Later, I was self-satisfied to learn he was mimicking a popular television advertisement I had never laid eyes on.

Another favorite television story from this same period in my life comes from good friends I used to visit. They had invented a low-tech but highly effective method of giving a thumbs-down to whatever program might be airing on television. The device was a small, empty box wrapped in twine with a long tail. Instructions were simple and easy to learn. At appropriate moments, one would throw the box in disgust at the television screen, and then simply reel it in by pulling on the box's tail, readying oneself for the next offense.

But after many years of not owning a television, when our older daughter was about six we gave in and bought a small Philco black-and-white television. (A few years ago, while cleaning out the attic, I came across it, still packed snugly in its original box. Although I couldn't fathom why anyone would want it, I donated it to the reuse center.) Like the allowance we gave to the girls every Saturday, we also allotted them a certain number of TV hours to spend, a small enough number to motivate them to choose carefully. When the girls were teenagers, I watched a few shows right along with them: *Buffy the Vampire Slayer* (which made me want to be back in high school if only to have Willow for a friend), *My So-Called Life* for its fresh honesty and a young Jared Leto to stare it, and the respectably reflective *Felicity*.

Later, when my career was in full swing and my husband and I lived by roughly the same TV restrictions we set for the kids, we watched a few shows that leaned toward the quirky, such as *Northern Exposure* and *3rd Rock from the Sun*. Plus, as a staple for smart, laugh-out-loud comedy and satire, for many years Rick and I switched on *Saturday Night Live* whenever we managed to stay up late enough. But over the years we have come to watch less and less television, until our TV time has dwindled to practically nothing, helped along by the limits of buying only basic cable TV and then dropping cable altogether. [After buying and moving to a different home in 2016, we bought a package deal that comes with cable, but the only notable difference is my husband now gets to watch his favorite sporting events.]

Recently I looked up some statistics about television watching in the U.S. According to the results of the June 2014 *American Time Use Survey Summary* conducted by the Bureau of Labor Statistics in the U.S. Department of Labor, watching television was the leisure activity that occupied the most time among survey recipients (2.8 hours per day), accounting for more than half of leisure time among survey respondents age fifteen and over (on average). This data point equates to 19.6 hours per week (the equivalent of a half-time job) or 1,019 hours per year–42.5 entire days of watching television.

I know, I know. There *is* good quality television programming out there, and I don't mean to judge people who enjoy TV. But as I think back to my frustration listening to a blaring television with no watchers, I realize I owe a big thank you to my stepmother. She, after all, is the one who started me down this path of asking whether sitting passively in front an electronic box was how I wanted to spend my time. My answer was and is a definite "no." I think it would be fascinating to see the good, long list of the many kinds of activities in which I've invested my time because I chose not to spend it watching television. Before closing, I offer you a short bit of advice from a magnet I gave to one of our daughters, which to this day is affixed to our refrigerator: *Bad TV Read a Book.*

Looking back on my childhood, even though I loved being my father's TV buddy, I loved even more our weekly trips to the public library in downtown Springfield where I would check out my next tall stack of books, as many as the library allowed. Very early in life, I became a serious booklover. I also loved creating special spaces where I would read, including, at one point, a "room" beneath my bed, which was ridiculously impractical because the bed was so low to the floor. At the same time, it was romantic–my girl cave. If, instead, over the course of my life I had spent a lot more time staring at television, it's hard to overestimate the ways I—and my life—would be different.

## *Questions to Ponder*

- On average, each week how many hours of television do you watch?
- After blocks of time watching television, how do you tend to feel? What's your energy level like? How engaged do you feel?
- What important things are you not doing because of the time you give to watching television?
- What trade-offs are you making, and is it worth it?
- What are the important activities you could give more time to if you were to deliberately watch less television?

CHAPTER 14

# Don't Do Dumb Things

OFTEN WHEN I'M walking down the stairs in our home, whether from the second floor to ground level or down to our Michigan basement with its hint of mustiness, I think of a friend. Many years ago, she and I worked in the same office. A few months after I left there for a new job, I heard she had broken not one but both ankles. I cringed to think of it.

As the story was told to me, she was walking down the stairs carrying a basket of laundry when she took what she was thought was the final step down except it wasn't. When she found air instead of the solid ground she was expecting, as the nursery rhyme goes my friend had a great fall. The colleague who told me the story said my friend handled the situation as well as anyone could, which didn't surprise me. By nature, she is upbeat, cheerful, and resilient.

So how do I segue into the lesson, "Don't Do Dumb Things" without suggesting in any way that what my friend did was dumb? To do so would be unfair and unkind. Most of us carry stuff up and down stairs. For this very reason, more and more of my fellow boomers are moving into single-level homes. We may not talk much about it, but we see the long (hopefully gradual) physical decline that stares us dispassionately in the face. Plus, we all make mistakes. An accident like the one my friend experienced could happen to anyone.

At the same time, though, her story became a learning experience for me that staked a claim in my brain and has never left. Her momentary lapse in attention, which happens to all of us, was a big deposit in my bank of *for heaven's sake, pay attention to what you're doing.* When it comes to stairs, I've reaped the benefits of this lesson by making it a habit to use hand railings, especially if I'm carrying something or when a feeling in the pit of my stomach tells me to hang on. Thanks to my friend, on countless occasions I have taken a split second to be sure I was at the bottom of the stairs before taking a step.

The title of this chapter comes from a book our older daughter and her husband recommended to me and to my husband, Mark Sisson's *The Primal Blueprint.* In his book, Sisson lays down an argument for continuing to live, at least in fundamental ways, like our primal ancestors. (Don't worry, this doesn't mean giving up your smartphone, although I'll touch on this point later.) In addition to information about following a Paleo diet, only some of which makes sense to me, Sisson offers up numerous lessons from our Paleolithic kin, which he calls *laws*. This chapter is based on Primal Blueprint Law #9, *Avoid Stupid Mistakes.*

Have I done dumb things in my life? (As I get ready to answer, can you feel the shudder going through my body?) Oh, yes. I'll give you just a few examples. When I was in my early twenties, several times I hitchhiked alone from southern to northern Vermont to see a boy. Fortunately, the worst thing that happened was when a truck driver groped at my breasts just before I was about to climb out. Even though hitchhiking was a lot more common back then, it was still a dumb thing to do. Ah, the foolish things we do in the name of love.

Then there was a night in the middle of winter in 1972 when I drove home from what was then the Red Baron, a restaurant and bar on Route 15 two miles south of Johnson, home of Johnson State College (soon to be Northern Vermont University–Johnson), where I earned my undergraduate degree. Having drank far too much beer and in no condition to be behind the wheel, as I drove the two miles back into town it came to me (with idiotic smugness) that all I needed to do to make it home without killing myself (or someone else) was to drive inside *both* sets of the lines my drunken double vision had put on the road.

Perhaps my scariest example of stupid behavior was the time I drove my 1963 purple-painted Volkswagen Beetle at top speed down the long hill heading north on Vermont's Interstate 91 between Bellows Falls and Springfield. With the radio blaring, my friend's sister and I, laughing at the tops of our lungs as we tore downhill at close to seventy miles per hour, pulled the sort of prank only undeveloped brains like ours could conjure–we *switched seats.* (Studies have shown the rational part of the brain isn't fully developed until age twenty-five, which, since I was only twenty-two at the time of this prank, might give me a shred of an excuse for being so foolish. Oy vey!)

When I tell these stories, I feel lucky to be alive.

Given these stories and others from my own life, I welcome the idea of an inner voice that whispers at me (and sometimes shouts), "Don't do dumb things." Dumb things, of course, are in the eye of the beholder. You would never find me ice climbing in Yosemite or racing downhill on a bicycle at fifty miles per hour. But while it would be dumb for *me* to do either of these things, I don't judge the people who thrive on these extreme sports. In many ways, I admire them. Instead, the short list of dumb things offered below is much more mundane. Their cautious nature probably shows my age, regardless of how biologically young I feel.

*1. It's dumb to be on your phone and drive at the same time.*

Okay, Bluetooth technology users, hands-free is different–maybe. Nevertheless, studies show that because the person on the other end of a cell phone *can't see what you see,* if something unexpected happens that screams for your complete attention, your friend isn't going to be much help (if any). To my list of related dumb things to do while driving I would add eating and singing while driving, both of which I do at times (no, not at the same time, which would be dumbness squared). Shame on me.

*2. When walking across the street (even at a crosswalk), it's dumb to put your safety in other people's hands.*

It is dumb to think that drivers in all directions see you and will necessarily avoid doing any of the many dumb things that could result in your vulnerable body being hit by a car. A couple of years ago in Ann Arbor, a scene unfolded on a busy four-lane road in a crosswalk that had been installed specifically to protect pedestrians. On both sides of the road next to the crosswalk, neon green signs with lights flashing (set off by a button pushed by the pedestrian) warn drivers to pay attention. Plus, a similar but even larger sign is suspended directly over the crosswalk. These highly visible signs almost shout at drivers to slow down.

That afternoon, a woman had crossed the two eastbound lanes of traffic, passed over the protective concrete island in the middle of the road, and continued to cross the road in front of a car stopped in the first westbound lane. But when, without looking, she stepped into the fourth and final lane, a car driven by another young woman hit her body with such force she flew like a ragdoll, landing with a sound no one who was anywhere near her at the time will ever forget. The driver's actions that day weren't just dumb; they were also criminal. Despite a completely clean record up to that point, she was sentenced to time in jail. With one life snuffed out (the woman who died that day was a university student in her prime) and the life of the driver who killed her changed forever, the accident was a tragedy in every way. Count me as a driver who has learned from this wrenching story to take extraordinary care at pedestrian crossings and intersections.

Plus, as a pedestrian, whenever I cross the street I look carefully in all directions before stepping into a crosswalk. I also believe bicyclists need to be equally cautious. Even if a driver is in the wrong, a bicyclist has so much more to lose. I hope my encounter with a bicyclist described below will help drive the point home.

Just a few days before writing this chapter, I drove down a side street to bypass a busy traffic light. At the end of the street, the road elbows to the left and ends at a stop sign with greatly restricted visibility. After stopping the car, I glanced up the short stretch of sidewalk on my right that, behind some dense shrubs, continues up over a bridge. Seeing no one, I checked to my left for traffic. Seeing nothing, I pulled forward into a right-hand turn. Suddenly, out of nowhere, I heard loud shouts of "Hey! Hey!"

Braking quickly, I turned my head to see an incensed bike rider, who must have been barreling down the sidewalk only seconds after I had glanced in that direction. Backing up to let him pass, I apologized to him several times through the open window. As he sped away, he continued to spew curses at me. Over the next few days I will replay the scene in mind, scaring myself badly with "what-if" scenarios.

That very day I added taking that shortcut to my dumb things list, and ever since, regardless of how much traffic is on the road or how much of a rush I'm in, rather than trying to shave a few seconds off my trip I dutifully join the line of cars at the traffic light, where, if traffic flow allows, it's safe to turn right on red.

As a point of contrast, two days later I drove into a post office lane in downtown Ann Arbor to mail some letters. The drive-up mailbox is at the end of the post office parking lot, where, because the street is one way, when pulling back into traffic drivers must make a sharp, right-hand turn. After dropping my letters in the slot, and with my experience with the bicyclist a few days earlier still fresh in my mind, I inched forward and then looked first to my left and then to my right. There, on my right only a few feet away, was a woman on a bicycle, waiting patiently to be sure I had seen her before she rode past. As I waved her forward, I say to myself *Smart move.*

Later, as I think back to the guy on the bike two days earlier, even if he did have the right of way I conclude that flying down that sidewalk on his bicycle into a semi-blind intersection was his own version of a dumb thing to do.

*3. It's dumb to not fasten your seatbelt.*

Before deciding once and for all to fasten our seatbelts and make a habit of it, how many more accidents must we read about where people not wearing their seatbelts are thrown violently from a car and killed? Because cars are such a big a part of our lives, it's easy to shove out of our minds the fact that automobile travel is incredibly dangerous. In 2012, more than 30,000 people died in motor vehicle crashes in the U.S. alone (Fatality Analysis Reporting System). This number compares to 800 people *worldwide* who died the same year in aircraft accidents (Bureau of Aircraft Accidents Archives), making travel by car more than thirty-seven times more dangerous than flying.

Yet most of us know people who are so petrified of flying they cannot step foot onto a plane. I know this type of thinking isn't rational, but in view of these statistics, logically it makes better sense for people to refuse, under any circumstances, to climb into a car. In my book, not wearing a seatbelt ranks up there at the top of a list of dumb things to do.

*4. It's dumb to not wear a bicycle helmet.*

Decades ago a good friend of mine was in a bad bicycle accident in which she went headfirst over the handlebars. As a result, over the years she has suffered tremendously from the repercussions of her injuries that day. Fortunately, she was wearing a bike helmet. One can only imagine how much worse off she might have been without it. She is yet another friend who taught me an important lesson. I will never ride my bike without a helmet no matter where I'm riding.

A few years ago, Rick and I spent a marvelous few days pedaling on the gravel carriage trails at Acadia National Park in Maine, where no vehicle traffic is allowed. Did we wear helmets on those automobile-free roads? We sure did. Even though most bicycle-related deaths occur in accidents involving motor vehicles, no matter where we ride, these heads of ours, despite hard skulls, are incredibly fragile.

Unfortunately, during the past few years, I've seen a discouraging trend–more and more bicyclists not wearing helmets. Having done a fair amount of bike riding, I know wearing a bike helmet isn't exactly fun. If the helmet fits properly (as in it could save your life if you fall or get hit), it's a bit tight under the chin. It's not especially comfortable on hot days when it makes one's head sweat. Plus, there's no real brim to keep the sun out of the eyes. But when bicyclists choose not to wear helmets, this decision flies in the face of hard evidence that helmets prevent serious injury and save lives. Unfortunately, as more people choose not to wear a helmet, it sends a message to other bicyclists that riding without a helmet must be okay. Bit by bit, unfortunate trends spread.

The Michigan legislators and governor have put freedom to ride a motorcycle without a helmet far above commonsense and strong evidence of more deaths and increased medical costs when riders go helmetless (which most of us end up paying for in one way or another). In my book, riding a motorcycle without a helmet is a decidedly dumb thing to do. Please, motorcycle-riding friends, even though there's no law in Michigan telling you to wear a helmet, do it anyway.

There are more things on my list of dumb things to do list but let's call it a day, shall we? And as soon as I save this file, I promise to take a few minutes to backup my hard drive. (I'll spare you that sad story.) Even with my backup, external drive, if there's a fire or someone breaks into the house and steals both the computer and the drive, where would I be then? Why in the world, you might reasonably ask, haven't I registered with an online backup company, especially when it's inexpensive, automatic, and so much more secure? Yes. You already know the answer. Like everyone else, I do dumb things.

## *Questions to Ponder*

- Can you think of any important lessons you've learned from "dumb things" you've done?
- What lessons have you learned from other people?
- What's one "dumb thing" you want to stop doing?

## CHAPTER 15

# Be a Steward of the Earth

THE DISPLAY OF photos and postcards on the front of our refrigerator, along with the magnets that affix them, are welcome bits of color against its pale white surface. Some of these mementos invite us to savor vacations past: Utah, Alaska, Vancouver Island. Others are picture-perfect postcards family members sent from Greece, Hawaii, Kenya, England. Best of all are the photographs. Most of the smiling faces that look out at us are family: parents, kids, nephews, and nieces. In my favorite a small black-and-white photo with ridged edges, my mother-in-law stands on a dock next to the water. She wears a dark, one-piece bathing suit. On her feet are low-heeled, slip-on shoes more like bedroom slippers, fashionable at the time, than like beach shoes. Her trim waist is the hourglass figure every woman yearns for, is afraid of losing, or remembers from the past.

In the mix is a photograph of Rick and me with our good friends, Bert and Kay. Ours is a friendship that was seeded and has grown over the years during only the few days each year when we meet on our respective annual pilgrimages to Stokely Creek Lodge in Goulais River, Ontario, a half-hour's drive northwest of Sault Ste. Marie, Canada. In the photo, the four of us scrunch next to each other like kids who worry the photo's edges will cut off some important part of themselves.

Although we only see our friends once a year, we feel very close to them. Perhaps it's the delight of crossing paths out on Stokely's web of groomed cross-country ski trails. When this happens, we chat for a few minutes about the sky, the weather, skiing conditions, or what the lodge might be serving for lunch that day, how good it will be to sit down to bowls of hot soup. Our cheeks flush from the cold, our exertion, and from good health. When our fingers grow cold from standing around, we ski off with a wave, delighted to have run into friends in this expanse of protected wilderness where we often ski for hours at a stretch without seeing a soul.

We see Stokely as a cross-country skier's paradise, which is saying a lot for two people who met and got married in the beautiful mountains of Vermont and plan to spend much more time there after my husband finishes his career. The resort's seventy miles of groomed, well-marked ski trails range from flat and easy to nail-biting steep, with names like Sayer Lake, Julie's, Jack Rabbit, Lower Dustin, Peterson's, and King Mountain. Except for the mild grinding of the grooming machines we sometimes hear nearby or that pass us on the trail after a snowstorm big enough to warrant the expense of re-grooming, the only sounds we hear are the wind in the trees, creaking branches, water making its way musically down the creek over rocks or under ice and snow, and the occasional, distant buzz of a small airplane.

One year not long ago, on a day in late September, Rick and I drove two hours to Indiana to visit our friends in a different season and different place, their beautiful lake-front home. After leaving the interstate, we drove by stands of trees that were slowly giving up their green to the glorious shades of fall. Although Indiana was no Vermont or even northern Michigan, the trees here nevertheless were hard at work. With shorter days, the steady upward flow of chlorophyll that painted them a deep summer green had given way to hidden splashes of brilliant orange, yellow, and red.

After we arrived, I was delighted to finally have the chance to stand in their kitchen looking out windows that offer a full view of the sky above the parade of cottages and summer homes on the western shore, perfect for savoring deep pink, cloud-laced sunsets. To the north grow the property's trees and shrubs and, just beyond, the elegant home where Kay's father's modest summer cabin once stood. (After Bert and Kay were married, when the cabin next to Kay's father's place came up for sale, they jumped at the chance to buy it as a summer home. This was the modest cabin they had razed just a few years earlier to make way for their new home.) Later we walked the well-worn path in the woods that link the two homes. Once, more than thirty years ago when two small cabins sat on these same lakefront lots, Kay and Bert's young daughter walked proudly by herself, unaware of her mother and grandmother, both watching carefully, protectively, standing back from the windows just far enough to let the girl feel proud of walking this path "completely on her own." I felt as if she could still be watching us from where she hid behind a tree as an impish smile lit up her face.

In my mind, I returned to a conversation our friends and I had after dinner one night a few years ago at Stokely when Bert told us, in almost a whisper, as if afraid to jinx their fledgling dream, about razing their small cabin to build a year-round home in its place, where they would live full-time after retiring, and after selling their year-round home located in south-central Michigan, where they had lived and worked for many years. During the forty plus years since they purchased the cabin, they spent time nearly every weekend there during the summer. So, at the time of our hushed conversation around a Stokely fireplace, it had been a shock for us to hear our friends, two people who lean toward maintaining the status quo, to be thinking of tearing down their beloved summer cabin, and to build, in its place, a house that would become their only home. Now, on the day of our visit to our friends' new home, there we were, my husband and I, years after the what-if conversation at Stokely, seeing firsthand the happy evidence of planning, hard work, and faith, the plunge taken, the dream brought to life.

In a tour of the lake in Bert's *Four Winns* boat with its Ford V-8 225-horsepower motor, we saw firsthand the rapidly changing nature of the shoreline. Small, modest cabins with their sweetly creaking screen doors stand humbly next to new three-story homes that stare back at us with eyes that tell the tale of a land with fewer trees, less open space, and little breathing room. Sadly, people call these character-rich small cottages "tear-downs." Their destiny, it seems, is to be bought at outlandish prices only for the land on which they now stand and where they have stood for a very long time. Their gentle sloping roofs, screen doors, small windows, and decades of carefree summer memories that infuse the walls and woodwork will follow the fate of other small cottages that new owners have obliterated. I turned to Bert to comment on these mammoth summer homes, and with a shrug he asked, "Why? Then again, with a sigh: "Why?"

Why do people want such large houses, especially for second homes? First, I must confess that at times I envy people who live in these houses with numerous amenities. Tuning into that envy, I venture a guess about why so many people build big. These large summer homes include plenty of bedrooms; dedicated guestrooms; a generous number of bathrooms; places to eat, prepare and store food; rooms for watching TV shows and movies, and playing video games; indoor fitness centers; screened porches for bug-free summer evenings; multi-car garages, and a plethora of closets and storage. Then there are such aesthetics as high, open spaces with lots of light. Finally, I see and understand the sense of pride and accomplishment that comes with owning such a home and being able to share it with others. In a nutshell, these large homes offer up comfort, convenience, pride, enjoyment, and beauty.

I expect, without a doubt, that many of these people (a good number of whom must surely be doctors, attorneys, business owners, bankers, or other professionals) work hard and probably for long hours. Some of them have probably given up many years of their lives to training and exhausting apprenticeships. In response to the question "Why?" they might just as reasonably counter by asking me "Why not?"

I reflect on the modest Cape Cod built in 1948 that Rick and I called home for almost thirty years. Despite good jobs, regular raises, promotions, and the option many times over of moving up, going bigger and better, we have stayed. Over the years most of the rooms became chameleon-like: when the need arose, we changed both their appearance and function. By turns, my office became a spare bedroom or fiber arts room. The upstairs bedroom doubled as a small fitness center (exercise bike, hand-held weights, yoga mat) and the place where we kept most of our clothing.

The family room downstairs was both dining room and living room. It was also the place where my husband, after moving a few chairs out of the way, did his strength and stretching routine almost every morning. In our galley kitchen, a mudroom/entrance bench sat at the east end and the southwest corner of this long room served as a compact breakfast nook, with a small glass-topped table and two metal cushioned stools. The basement housed an assortment of plastic bins that held linens, kayaking equipment, camping equipment, extra towels, boxes of our daughters' childhood things they're not yet ready to let go of, quilting fabrics, knitting supplies, toiletries we only need occasionally, tools, garden seeds, extra office supplies, and more.

Why did we stay so long in the same house, despite having the wherewithal to "move up?" Because we believe it is important not to ask just "Why?" but just as importantly to ask, "Why not?" Why not build large? Why not go for bigger? Why not more? If we will but take the time to ask the question and listen, the answers come from the earth itself. The many conveniences of our lives hide the ways we daily use up the earth's resources. Being able to drive easily into a gas station to fill up our cars, getting to choose between multiple products when we need something, moving the thermostat up in winter and down in summer without a second thought—the list of conveniences we take for granted seem endless. At a hellish pace we are, quite simply, using up the earth's unspeakably precious resources that were created over many eons.

I confess at times I envy people with more than one bathroom. Yes, it would be nice to have a dedicated guestroom. If we move again, for sure we'll have a second bathroom or at least a half-bath. But beyond that, neither of us wants more. Furthermore, we believe it is a good thing to use individual rooms for several purposes, a direction that, as citizens of this splendid earth, we surely need to move toward over time. We also keep a compost pile year-round (even though a trip out to the compost bin behind the garage in subzero weather is nobody's idea of fun), recycle everything we can, keep things going for as long as possible rather than buy new, limit how much stuff we buy, take the bus instead of drive. Like our friends Bert and Kay, we do our best to be good stewards. Do we do enough? Never. Despite our efforts to conserve the earth's resources, do we use more than our fair share of the earth's resources? Guilty as charged. But at the same time, we contribute in some small way to the solution by asking, when tempted by the pull of "more" and when we catch ourselves envying other people, the essential question "Why?"

Back from the tour of the lake with Captain Bert, I appreciate even more our friends' decision to limit their footprint on this small piece of land. I respect the gentle path that leads through "the swamp" and the small stream whose minerals color the earth rust brown as it runs downhill, entering the lake near the table where Bert regularly cleans the fish he and his grandson catch in the rowboat as their lines trail behind them while they talk and laugh in the way only a five-year-old and his grandfather can. I feel deeply the emotional, even visceral pain our friends experienced as they gave the builders the go-ahead to cut down two large trees to make way for their larger home.

Little wonder we have formed this friendship that deepens every year over only a few days in February, over meals shared family style, hours spent around the fireplace, over the rare times when we run into each other on the trails, cheeks and noses painted a healthy red by the cold, and over hours spent after dinner in our own worlds, reading. What binds us together? It's our values, our ways of being in the world. Just one example is the careful way our friends planned and designed their home. They, too, asked important questions: *What kind of spaces do we really need? How can we minimize the house's footprint on the land? What's most important?*

Early on Sunday afternoon, we climbed into the car, ready to drive back up the gravel road after saying goodbye to our friends. Next door a small dog barked as fierce a sendoff as it could muster. Standing in the driveway, our friends smiled and waved. At six foot three, Bert towers over Kay. But to my eyes, each are giants in spirit, deeply respectful of the land they live on and the lake they look gratefully out on each day. In asking "why?" they are the very kind of stewards the earth so badly needs.

*Postscript.* Despite feeling good about living in our modest home in Ann Arbor, finally I had to escape the sounds of ever-busier traffic on the street where we lived, which, despite being a two-lane road with only a twenty-five-miles per hour speed limit, is an ever more heavily travelled artery in and out of the city. Our new home does, indeed, have two bathrooms and a separate guestroom. I was, though, sad to leave the little home we loved so well for almost thirty years. Plus, in every way possible, we continue to do our best to be good stewards of the earth in how we live. We were pleasantly surprised to discover, for example, that in our new, larger (and better-insulated) home we use less energy than in our former home.

## *Questions to Ponder*

- What's one habit or behavior of yours that nudges your conscience to ask yourself *why?*
- What does it mean to you to be a steward of the earth?
- What's one tangible way for you to be a more committed steward of the earth?

III

# Challenges—Gotta Love 'Em

Lions and tigers, and bears, oh, my!

–L. Frank Baum, *The Wonderful Wizard of Oz*

Life is always a tightrope or a feather bed. Give me the tightrope.

–Edith Wharton

CHAPTER 16

# Allow Yourself a Rolling Personal Best

For six of the past eight years, on the first Sunday in June my husband Rick has completed a half marathon, having joined hundreds of runners and walkers, many of them locals and most from Michigan, in the Dexter-Ann Arbor Run. The run, which also includes 10K and 5K runs/walks, first took place in 1974 to help celebrate Ann Arbor's 150-year anniversary. Much of the run's route follows the twists and turns of Huron River Drive, giving up inspiring views of the river for which it's named. I've often wondered how the race escaped being named after the beautiful winding river itself.

A full five months before each race, Rick begins to train. Like many competitive runners, by which I mean he takes running seriously and strives to do his best, he has his own personal training system and runs regularly with a group of local runners.

His training regimen, which includes the steps described here, verges on science. On specific days, he runs a predetermined number of miles, adding more over time. On the advice of some professional runners that he picked up as part of his ongoing learning of running techniques to improve his regimen, he has incorporated short walking intervals into his runs, and also tracks his heart rate. A few weeks before the race, he takes his longest run. Sometimes, toward the end of his training he runs a half-marathon whose course follows trails in the woods, just for fun but also to put in the miles. Two weeks before the race, he begins to shorten his runs to store energy for the big event. He continues to eat well, sleep well, and look forward to the big day. On the night before the race, he's especially mindful of what he eats.

When race day arrives, he wakes early to stretch, then mixes up a special drink that will fuel his muscles immediately after the race, as he recovers from more than thirteen miles of pushing his body. He places his wrist-worn GPS on the kitchen windowsill for it to connect to the satellites that will track his location. This high-tech tracker seems like a distant relic of Dick Tracy's two-way wrist radio.

That race day, I proudly served as my husband's one-woman support team. We drove to Dexter and waited in a long line to park the car. As the famous theme song from *Rocky* blared from enormous speakers, we joined the hundreds of runners and spectators that milled around Dexter High School as the runners stretched, shook out their legs, and nervously talked and laughed. The long lines at the porta potties grew longer as start time approached. Next to the brick school building sat a small tent top resting on four poles, marked with a large ELITE sign. The whole time we were there, not one runner approached it. I told Rick he was elite in my book and asked him to stand beneath it so I could take his photo. He declined.

As the clock to race time quickly approached, I gave my husband a kiss and walked to the start line, where, at the front of the pack, a group of runners, who could have legitimately stood beneath the tent for elites, continued to warm up their leg muscles, eager for the race to finally begin. When the ear-splitting horn sounded the start, the head runners set their watches and took off at a blistering pace they would sustain for the next hour or so.

Hoping to spot Rick as he ran by in the crowded mass of runners, I videotaped the entire start. The runners came by in waves, many of them clustered near the pacers who held tall signs with the pace they would carefully maintain throughout the race: average time per mile on the front side and finish time on the back. It would later take me at least fifteen minutes of stopping and starting the video to find Rick crossing the starting line. That day, he aimed for a finish time of two hours, a very respectable time for a guy who had only started running when he was well into his fifties and, at the time of the race, was on the upper side of the sixty to sixty-four age group.

As I headed back to the car, a voice from the loud speakers gave a final warning for any runners who hadn't yet started the race and who wanted their running times to be official. In the bib of each of the runners was a small chip that would record their start time. The same chip would capture their finish down to the hundredths of a second 13.1 miles downriver, just past the grueling half-mile uphill stretch that fed into a chute of waiting, cheering onlookers on Main Street in the heart of downtown Ann Arbor, where I drove to join them.

After I parked the car and found a good spot near the finish line, I watched hundreds of people running and walking by. Small orange cones split the street into two lanes: one side for the green-bibbed 5K runners and walkers and the other for the yellow-bibbed 10K entrants. Many spectators at the metal barricades on each side of the street craned their necks as they looked for family members, friends, or fellow runners. At just past an hour after the start of the half- marathon, race organizers funneled the 5K and 10K participants into the same lane, clearing the other one for the imminent arrival of the half-marathoners.

At an hour and seven minutes on the race clock, the lead half-marathoner flew by with arms and legs pumping like a well-oiled, elegant machine. *Good for him* I said to myself, as I applauded loudly and let out a few whoops. Later, I learned that he was thirty-eight, an impressive age to be leading a small pack of guys in their early twenties. The runner closest to him was a minute behind and the next one came by a good three minutes later. The top woman half-marathoner, who also happened to be thirty-eight, came in at just after an hour and seventeen minutes. As she ran by, my chest swelled and tears sprang to my eyes. (This reaction may seem a little over the top, but I'm also a woman who cries when I watch sappy television commercials.) The marathon runners, men and women, arrived in a trickle, then in small clumps, and eventually in a steady flow.

As I loudly cheered on the half-marathon lead runners, the long line of 10K and 5K participants–single people, couples, runners, walkers and people pushing strollers or wheelchairs–continued to pass by in the other lane. As I turned more of my attention to this wildly diverse group, I spotted one of my girlfriends, and then another. Faces red from exertion, they wore determined expressions. I hooted, called out their names, and, once I had their attention, pumped my fists into the air. Tuning into my belief that the only *real* runners there were the half marathoners, a sense of shame washed over me.

Although I continued to cheer on the half-marathon runners, I also applauded the 5K and 10K runners and walkers on the other side of the street. Although the top runners in these races had already received their medals and prize money and were likely on their way home already, the men, women, and children in front of me with much more modest goals had just as much of a right to feel proud as they crossed the finish line

They were a motley crew, some of them red-faced and panting, many of them overweight. Some walked slowly, as if they had nowhere special to go and all the time in the world to get there. Some were like hares, digging deep to sprint for the finish line, shaving off a few seconds from their times. Others kept a more tortoise pace ... almost there ... almost there ... almost there. The more I watched them, the more I admired them.

Back at the house, when Rick discussed his time with me, he told me about his notion of a rolling personal best, a concept he invented that takes into account that even the fittest bodies slow down over time, but can build muscle at any age, Rick's best time in the DXA2 was from his first race, when he was fifty-eight. But, he explained, he had decided to calculate his personal best or personal record (PR) based on his times from only the five most recent races. With this formula, each year an earlier race time dropped out of the math.

What a fine idea, I told him, one that could be applied to all sorts of activities or realities. (Maybe, I thought, I could apply this notion even to such things as the dimpled texture of the skin on my upper arms and neck, which no amount of fitness work was likely to improve. Now there's a good thought, seeing the condition of my skin in terms of my "personal best.") As I thought about the people I had heretofore labeled as "stragglers," I decided to stop using this miserly, mean-spirited term. They were not stragglers. They were making the effort. They were challenging themselves on their own terms, and doing their best.

In my mind, I committed to cheering them on as if each of them were the lead man or woman in the half-marathon. They deserved a personal best whatever it might be, and the older ones deserved the bonus of a rolling personal best. Go runners! Almost there! Looking good!

## *Questions to Ponder*

- What does "personal best" mean to you? Could it be about quantity as well as quality?
- What's one thing in your life you've judged yourself for as you slow down or are less successful at over time?
- How might you give yourself the gift of a rolling personal best in this situation?
- How could you use the concept of a rolling personal best to view yourself and your efforts, as you get older, in a more positive light?

CHAPTER 17

# There *Is* Life After Running

IN A PHOTOGRAPH taken by my brother Peter on a fine summer day in the late 1980s, I stood alone at the summit of Vermont's Mount Pisgah above Lake Willoughby, gazing out on the rippled lake below. Just a few minutes after my brother snapped the photo, I slid on some loose dirt on the hike back down and jackknifed my right knee, and then I limped my way back to the car. Too stubborn to see a doctor, I patiently waited out the two months it took for me to return to my longstanding practice of running three miles three times a week.

But ten years later, on another fine summer day while out jogging, a sudden, severe pain in my right knee stopped me up short. I had no choice but to walk home. When the pain persisted, I saw my doctor and then an orthopedic surgeon who later saw me for a second appointment to discuss my x-rays. Drawing a circle around the outside section of my right knee on a photocopy of the x-ray, he explained, "See this thin line? It means the cartilage there has worn down completely." He explained that my injury years ago had damaged the anterior ligament, after which the knee no longer tracked in a straight line. Each time my foot had hit the ground during my runs, my cartilage had worn away, bit by tiny bit. The doctor paused with a sigh and added, "When cartilage is gone, it's gone." Nothing, including surgery, could fix it.

His bad news knocked the wind out of me. I heard the clear message beneath his words: *your running days are over*. While in his office and in the days and weeks to come, I cried and grieved. For people who love to run, giving it up is like losing a close friend. I will always miss running and feel the loss.

Over the years since my knee brought my running to an abrupt halt, my husband has assumed the position of runner in the family. As of this writing, he has run five half-marathons, and a couple of months ago completed his first marathon at age sixty-five (having since added a second one). Before Rick's races, when I go with him to registration sites where runners pick up their bibs and other information, my status as a mere bystander never fails to choke me up. At the same time, I stand in awe of my husband's dedication to the art and science of running. Despite years as a dedicated runner, I was never in his league. (I participated in just one race, a 6K in 1978). With a great deal of discipline, he has earned every one of his race medals. I'm proud of his accomplishments and even more of his hard work and effort.

Over the years, I have managed to slowly let go of my identity as a runner. I now take a brisk walk Monday through Saturday, and a more leisurely, longer walk with Rick on Sundays. I have come to believe that for most people, walking is the best exercise there is. Because walking doesn't give me as high a level of cardio workout as running, three days each week I also ride a stationary bike in a workout that includes three one-minute sprints spaced out over my half-hour ride. (Some call this cardiovascular exercise strategy high intensity interval training. If you would like to do this kind of training, it's important to talk with your doctor.) For me, bicycle sprints are only a small part of an overall exercise regimen and active lifestyle that brings me much pleasure.

The bottom line is that although it was a big challenge for me to give up running, I moved through the typical stages of grief, and eventually came around to stop fighting internally over what I couldn't do and focus instead on what I *could* do.

## *Questions to Ponder*

- In your life, are there activities (not necessarily related to physical exercise) you have had to give up akin to my having to give up running?

- What have you learned from your experience?
- If you're having a hard time making the transition, what can you do to move yourself closer to accepting what is, while also staying true to who you are and what's important to you?

CHAPTER 18

# When the Way Is Challenging (Some) Ignorance Is Bliss

When my husband and I met it became immediately clear we both loved the outdoors, especially wild places. This mutual passion has translated into many different outdoor activities, but the first hikes we enjoyed on mountain trails near where we lived in northern Vermont began to strengthen the bond between us. But after my knee diagnosis, strenuous hiking was seemingly off the table.

But things took a welcome turn on one of our trips to Vermont to see friends and family and to enjoy the parade of fall colors. As we planned for the trip, Rick convinced me to try hiking the challenging top section of Mt. Mansfield, at 4,395 feet the tallest of the Green Mountains. Knowing my bad knee story, you'll understand that for me this would mean a challenge unlike any I had dared since the orthopedic physician delivered his heart-wrenching news.

Since Rick had a special affinity with Mt. Mansfield (having skied it nearly every day for several winters as a ski patrol member at Stowe) and he enjoyed hiking solo sometimes, the day before our planned hike he decided to hike the entire mountain, a six- to seven-hour trip that begins where the Long Trail crosses the road in Underhill, leading to the Mt. Mansfield summit and then follows a different trail down to complete a sweeping loop. The free day gave me time to travel with my brother and sister-in-law to the small Vermont town where our parents grew up, where we visited an uncle (the only surviving family member of my parents' generation) and his wife, of whom we are quite fond.

The next day, Rick and I drove up the historic Toll Road to the base of the gondola lift at Stowe Mountain Resort. Alone in our cab, we softly clunked past each tower on the gondola's stiff climb to the Cliff House. Most of the riders simply enjoy the soul-soothing views of the ridges, peaks, valleys, and rivers that stretch into the distance, have lunch in the restaurant, and visit the gift shop before climbing into one of the gondola cabins for the ride back down the mountain to the sprawling parking lot below.

For us, though, arrival at the Cliff House was just the beginning of our afternoon trek. After getting our bearings, we found the signpost marking the beginning of the Cliff Trail, a connector leading up to the Long Trail, which winds along the ridgeline on top of the mountain. Because of my knee, I was nervous about the hike. My anxiety stayed high when the climb up the trail immediately proved to be harrowing, at least for me. We clamored up boulders stacked almost end to end like a rough-hewn river of rock. I proceeded cautiously, slowly behind Rick. At one point, the trail forced us to stoop down and scoot up through a small space beneath a particularly large boulder. From atop the boulder, I looked behind me, breathed a sigh of relief, and then turned back to the trail to resume taking step after careful step.

When we finally reached the intersection of the Long Trail at the end of the Cliff Trail, the worst was behind us. Rick pointed out the two ridges he had followed the day before, up one and down the other. Whereas the south ridge was covered in thick forest, the north ridge was a big-boned cascade of sheer rock, aptly named Sunset Ridge because of its breathtaking views to the west. We then resumed our hike on a much easier trail up to the summit of the Chin. (From a distance, the Mt. Mansfield peaks appear to carve a long, distinguished face looking up at the sky, one with a distinct forehead, nose, lips, chin, and Adam's apple.)

On the top of the mountain, we had lots of company as we took in the phenomenal 360-degree views of New Hampshire's White Mountains to the east, New York's Adirondacks to the west across Lake Champlain, Quebec to the north, and, stretching downstate, the mountains that are my familiar companions whenever I drive south on I-89 toward my hometown. When we had taken our fill of the views and our packed lunch, we headed back down, following an easier route. Without incident, we made our way back at the parking lot. Before I climbed into the car, I paused to look once more toward the top of the mountain. As I gazed upward, a warm glow of satisfaction filled my chest.

Perhaps the most important part of this story, though, is what I learned on our drive back to Burlington. My husband told me that on his solo hike, he happened to reach the intersection at the Cliff Trail just as a woman was finishing the climb. When he asked her what the trail was like, she answered, "Frightening!" and then added, while casting a worried look, "My husband is still down there." While buying our gondola tickets earlier, Rick had picked up a trail brochure. Reading it, he noticed the Cliff Trail's climb rating: DDD, the highest level of difficulty. Knowing how I might react, he had quietly folded the brochure and slid it into his back pocket. Because he believed I could make the climb, he didn't want to risk having me think any differently.

What was the lesson from this experience? Sometimes it's best not to know *too* much about the path in front of us (within reason, of course). While planning a trip to the southern hemisphere, a good friend said several people she spoke with about her plans were quick to share their negative experiences. I'm a firm believer in good planning that takes into account possible obstacles or problems. But when it comes to telling others about my bad experiences, I prefer to share only specific advice or information I wish I had known beforehand. We all have good and bad luck, and bad luck for me (or good) doesn't mean someone else will have the same experience. For example, on a trip to Alaska, because of forest fires burning upwind my husband and I saw precious little of Denali's 20,000-foot peaks through the haze, a great disappointment. But a few years later, friends of ours found the bluest of skies, crisp air, and crystal-clear views. Rick did me a wise turn, I believe, to withhold the "bad news" he had heard about the Cliff Trail.

My lesson had its limits, though. Had it been raining the day my husband and I planned to climb the Cliff Trail, I would not have attempted it. At times in life we step boldly; at other times, we move more mindfully, even cautiously. Sometimes, though, it may be best simply to head out and find our way, one step at a time, toward the destinations we choose. This truth applies to a lot more than to actual DDD trails (or to any trails we see that way). Only by stepping past the signpost at the trailhead do we open ourselves up to the possibility of enjoying the views that await us at the top and, more importantly, to knowing the deep satisfaction of having achieved our goal.

## *Questions to Ponder*

- What types of challenging trails in life are unnecessarily holding you back?
- Who do you need to be to find, metaphorically, the appropriate signpost for whatever type of climb you want to take and, despite your misgivings, head up the trail?

CHAPTER 19

# Keep Pushing Your Limits

IN OCTOBER 2013, Rick and I drove to Vermont to visit family, take in the fall foliage, and begin looking for a house to buy or some land to build on.

Wednesday morning, my husband and I woke early. Following my success two years earlier climbing the Cliff Trail, at Rick's urging I had agreed to take on the bigger challenge of climbing to the top of Camel's Hump, the third highest mountain in Vermont, a hike I had always wanted to do.

The night before the hike I had a restless night, haunted by bad dreams of being unable to maneuver up or down the mountain. The nightmare brought back memories of the only time my husband took me downhill skiing, on a small mountain that was then called Little Spruce at Stowe Mountain Resort. Without having had a single lesson and with almost no experience, I had stood at the edge of the trail for what felt like an hour, my skis safely parallel to the mountain. Looking down, I watched other skiers fly by, certain my cost for skiing down the mountain would involve broken bones. (Although I managed to make it without hurting myself, that day marked the end of my downhill skiing.) Despite my bad dream and the fact that a few years earlier I would have considered this climb to be out of the question, that day I was fully on board to climb to Camel's Hump peak. What had changed?

For one thing, I had hard-earned faith in my physical ability to make this climb. After learning a few years earlier about the worn cartilage in my right knee, I had included in my workouts a list of exercises I've received over the years from physical therapists and other health care providers, designed to strengthen the muscles surrounding my knees. To increase my ability to push, pull, and lift (recommended ways to compensate for a bad knee), I also work diligently on my upper body strength. In addition, I've collected a few important strategies for favoring a bum knee, such as this one: when stepping up, lead with the healthy knee, when stepping down, lead with the injured one. In summary, I had invested a great deal in my body (and in myself) and decided now was the time to test the results with this challenging hike.

After we strapped on our daypacks, we took the first steps of our planned 5.8-mile loop that began at the trailhead parking lot in Camel's Hump State Park. Like even the most experienced hikers, I entered the woods and followed the trail one step at a time. At particularly steep or challenging places, I gave myself full, unembarrassed permission to play it safe. Sometimes I scooted up or down on my butt. Other times, I retraced my steps to find what looked like an easier or safer route. Often, I took my husband's advice. When we reached the summit, dotted with clusters of hikers on that gorgeous fall day, we paused to enjoy a lunch of fruit, cheese, salami, crackers, and almonds. My happiness and the sense of satisfaction I felt with my progress and the beautiful day were palpable.

Because of my knee injury, though, the greatest challenge was still in front of me, as hiking down would be the hardest part for my knees. As we descended, I was extra cautious, keeping a slow pace. Fortunately, this part of the trail wasn't as steep or rugged as the trail we'd climbed earlier. When we reached the easy, lower part of the trail, the same path we had hiked earlier that morning, I breathed an audible sigh of relief. Before long, we spotted the parking lot through the trees.

On our drive into town, I shot several backward glances at the top of the mountain, each time feeling another rush of pride from having met the challenge I set for myself. I thought back to those many years earlier when I stood on the side of a trail on Little Spruce, petrified to ski down. Although I'm delighted Rick and I switched to cross-country skiing, perhaps, I say to myself, I quit too soon. Part of me yearns for a do-over. I see now, for example, it was a mistake to ride the chairlift to a place on the mountain that I lacked the skiing ability to tackle. With the investment of a few lessons and some experience on the bunny hills, I felt sure I could have learned to look down that mountainside without heart-pounding fear and to have enough confidence to point my skis downhill, to give myself over to gravity with enough skill to control my speed, to make it down safely and enjoy the ride along the way.

What are the lessons from this story? Whether climbing a strenuous mountain trail, skiing a hill that feels impossibly steep, or undertaking any other activity that's a challenge, we would be wise not to underestimate ourselves, but instead to invest in ourselves, to open ourselves to what might be, to do what we *can* do when rather than judging ourselves, to seek out the resources we need to succeed, or at least to make a good go of it.

## *Questions to Ponder*

- What are the challenging trails in life that you are perhaps mistakenly holding yourself back from?
- What do you need to do, and who do you need to be, to find the appropriate signpost and, despite your misgivings, begin your climb?
- If fear is holding you back from doing something you would like to do, what type of investments in yourself would it take to alleviate that fear, to allow you to move forward?

## CHAPTER 20

# Lessons from the Screen House

For as far back as I can remember, I have yearned, at a visceral level, to live in a home with a screened porch. My desire was born when as kids, my brother Peter and I spent time at "camp." Our uncle and aunt owned three small cabins on Lake Groton, a short drive from the small town where my parents grew up. The main cabin, where we slept, had a lakeside screened porch, as most did back then and many still do. I can still hear the screen door slam, the latch gripping it in place, ready for the next kid to come in (or out) on the way to or from the dock and beach, where my brother, cousins, and I swam and played for hours, aware of time passing only when our stomachs began to growl, chasing us inside to clamor for something to eat.

The rub of screened porches though is that they cut down on the light coming into the house, and as anyone who has been in our home knows, my husband and I place a high premium on natural light. The western side of the home we owned in Ann Arbor, which faced the backyard (an add-on to the original house), had generous windows on all three sides. Some years after buying the house, we had added an extra 100 square feet to that part of the house, more windows, and a sliding glass door that opened to a deck at floor level, where we ate most of our meals in the summer, weather permitting. We briefly discussed the possibility of turning the deck into a screened porch but were unwilling to sacrifice any of the light that poured directly into the house. So, in the summer of 2010 when Rick drew up sketches for a stand-alone screen house that he proposed building in our backyard's northwest corner, I was thrilled. It was the perfect solution. (Although most people would probably call our structure a gazebo, because of its more modern architectural design my husband and didn't like that term—hence the name screen house. Later, when it came time to list the house for sale, our Realtor decided to call it a lanai. So, take your pick!)

That fall, in the project's first phase, Rick pulled up the grass, leveled the site, and put in a simple foundation. On top of it, he built a cedar floor. Over the winter, we joked about our private snow-covered dance floor. With winter and spring behind us, and after Rick had purchased or received delivery of the necessary materials, on a Saturday morning early in June, he was ready to begin. His ambitious goal was to finish the screen house by the time he returned to work only ten days later.

Most people will attest that it almost always takes us longer to complete any project than we first imagine. My husband, though, was hell bent on completing this project in as short a time as possible. For one thing, he wanted us to be able enjoy the screen house that summer. Plus, our thirty-fifth-wedding anniversary was less than a month away, and he meant the screen house to be an anniversary gift for both of us.

As Rick's main helper, I simply assumed he would need to find someone else to help him with the heavy lifting, especially when it came time to lift the four 8 x 8-inch cedar beams into place at each of the four corner posts and, afterward, to lift the sheets of plywood onto the rafters that would form the underside of the roof. I may be in good shape, I told myself, but there was no way I could do that kind of lifting. But not far into those first long workdays, I found myself at the other end of one of those beams lifting it into place. By day's end, both horizontal beams were in place and ready for the joists my husband would nail down to form the roof.

When I stepped back to see how the building was taking shape, I had a deep feeling of satisfaction, knowing that my (relatively) strong arms had helped make it happen. Within a few days, the two of us lifted the plywood sheets to create the roof, made easier by the scaffolding Rick built. And with that, the heavy lifting was done.

Lest you get the wrong idea, I must clarify that my husband did almost *all* the work on the screen house. Although I helped at times, and *only* when asked (one of the rules we observe in our relationship), my husband would probably say my biggest contribution was honoring his request not to ask him the endless line of questions my curiosity churns out like widgets off a production line, which, believe me, wasn't easy.

What made it possible for me to be Rick's only helper on this project? One factor was my long-standing commitment to staying strong and fit, in addition to being so active. But beyond just physical strength, there was another important force at work during that week the screen house came to life. Rick believed—indeed, *knew*—I was strong enough to help him with whatever work needed to be done. (This is just one of about a hundred reasons I'm still happily married to this fine man.) I believe his faith in me put me in a "do it anyway" frame of mind. *Think you can't handle it? Do it anyway.*

Less than a month after my husband began building the screen house, on a blistering hot day in July it was just about done. While shooting a short video of Rick squeezing the trigger of his electric drill to put in the final screws on the door hinges, I asked him, in my best Barbara Walters imitation, "So how does it feel to be putting in the last screws?" With the back of his dark sleeveless shirt drenched in sweat, he answered, "It feels hot." When I laughed, insisting he must be at least a little excited about being almost done, he said flatly, "No. Not excited. Just hot."

On July ninth that year, we celebrated our anniversary with dinner for two in the screen house. How sweet it was! For the remaining years we lived in that house, on summer mornings after I finished my exercise routine, sometimes I ambled out to the screen house, a cup of steaming tea in hand. There, I let the creaking door slam lightly behind me, sat on one of the two wicker rockers that fit the space perfectly, and looked out through the screens at the southern sky. Even though the screen house was not on a lake, suddenly I felt like a kid again, on vacation. As I rocked my chair back and forth slowly with a smile on my face, I was thrilled to finally have our unique version of a screened "porch" and proud of having been my husband's only helper, for having *done it anyway.*

## *Questions to Ponder*

- Can you think of a time when you surprised yourself by believing yourself incapable of doing some action but doing it anyway? What did you learn from that experience?
- Is there something you want to do but that you lack faith in yourself to do? What's holding you back? What might need to shift inside for you to open yourself up to possibility?

CHAPTER 21

# Look for Traces of a Traildog In You

WHEN MY HUSBAND and I met and then fell in love, one of the things that drew us together—and has only grown stronger over the years–was our love of the outdoors, especially hiking. He lived in Waterbury Center on Route 15, just a few miles southwest of Stowe, Vermont, while I lived and worked in Johnson, which I drove to and from by a shortcut that skirted around the town of Morrisville. Hiking on trails in the Mount Hunger range was one of the activities that showed us quickly how much we had in common.

After forty years of marriage, I couldn't tally all the places we've hiked, so I'll offer up just a few examples. In 1977, six weeks after our wedding in early July, my husband and I took a three-week, delayed honeymoon trip that we tacked onto our move to Oregon, where I would complete my master's degree. During the trip, we hiked through such places as alpine meadows in the Tetons and the sparse, haunting beauty of the Badlands of North Dakota, where one morning we unzipped our tent to see buffalo grazing nearby.

When our older daughter was born less than two years later, we introduced her to hiking when she was just a few weeks old. After we zipped her into a blue corduroy baby carrier and strapped her securely to my husband's chest, we hiked up a butte just south of Eugene. For the whole trip Brenna slept soundly. In 1980, as part of our plans to take a meandering drive home to Vermont, we bought a used but pristine van whose customized interior made it almost easy to travel with a baby. At various places on the way we stopped to do some hiking, which included introducing our daughter to the inimitable Grand Canyon.

In the summer of 1982, we pulled up stakes again for a move to Ames, Iowa, where our younger daughter was born in the middle of the three years it took for Rick to complete his undergraduate degree in architecture. While we came to appreciate many of Iowa's features, including its big sky, during our three years there, we put our love for hiking mostly up on a shelf. With our move to Michigan for Rick to earn his master's degree, we brought it down again, as we explored many hiking trails across the state, as well as in the nearby Canadian province of Ontario. While the girls were growing up, we spent part of many summer vacations camping in Ontario's Lake Superior Provincial Park and hiking many of its trails. On these visits, we almost always walked this park's well-traveled, gentle trail that hugged the banks of the tumbling Sand River. Over the years on repeat visits, as the girls grew we added more strenuous hiking, including the trail to the top of the mountain that looks out over Old Woman Bay.

After the girls left home, we began to travel further afield on trips that always included hiking. One year we made our way, hand over hand, in Utah's Zion National Park along the chain firmly anchored to the narrow spine of the Bright Angel Trail that had terrifying drops of a thousand or more feet on each side. A few days later, we drove to Bryce Canyon National Park where, on one of our mornings there, with a light dusting of snow on the ground we stepped down into the hoodoo-filled majesty of the well-named Fairyland Trail—our first experience of the reverse climb—down, then up.

Although an avid hiker for many years, it was only while reading "Dog Years: Who Builds Those Thousands of Miles of Park Trails and How Do They Do It?" an article by Christine Byl in *National Parks Magazine,* that I woke up to how much I had taken for granted the many men and women (mostly volunteers) who blaze new trails and do the difficult and dirty work of maintaining the existing ones. Reading Byl's article, I was especially interested to learn about a breed of these rugged individuals who have successfully completed a rite of passage that gives them license to call themselves *traildogs.*

A traildog is a person who has worked with a professional trail crew for at least seven seasons (count them, *seven*), each of which must include being part of a crew for at least *four* months. The year they fulfill these criteria is when they receive their "dog year." In her article Byl laid out a few traildog principles, including "Work until you drop, and then a little longer."

At first glance, another principle, "Keep your chain saw sharp," may seem a little less applicable to us regular folks, but there's a lesson buried there, depending on how we use chainsaw as a metaphor. For example: back up your computer, take care of your body, and when the tornado sirens sound, for heaven's sake head for the basement instead of continuing to wash the dishes or nap on the coach.

Mulling over the chief characteristics of a traildog, I have guessed my way to five such traits.

*1. The only place where traildogs are fully themselves is the natural world.*
Given how deeply satisfying traildogs find the difficult, dirty work they do, they wear their worn, grubby clothes and muddy boots with pride. In this we all can find wisdom. Efforts to protect the natural world acknowledges and honors the precious and fragile interdependence we share with the earth. It also reminds us that we are first and foremost stewards who, especially given the nature and tendencies of being human, bear a responsibility to protect and preserve it. Lots of us, including me, tell ourselves we *should* step up the plate and help with this important, demanding work. Trail dogs do it.

*2. Traildogs are, yes, doggedly committed to the work they do.*
Working alongside park professionals and an army of people they call *hobbyists,* traildogs play a pivotal part in creating and maintaining the enormous web of hiking trails that cover the country. (Hobbyists are volunteers who work on trails but who aren't committed–or crazy–enough to pursue traildog status.)

Without these trails, millions of men, women, and children would miss the chance to venture into and become closely connected to the natural world, the place to best discover, savor, and hold experiences that are a big part of what makes us human. Plus, without maintained trails this mass of humanity drawn to the natural world would leave behind a great deal of destruction.

*3. Traildogs dig deep.*
Trail dogs work hard and they do it hour after hour, day after day, and month after month, digging, stooping, and carrying and wielding chainsaws. They cut brush, move rock, haul gravel, and tackle other backbreaking work. When they stop for a simple but large lunch, they are ravenously hungry. Then they're back at it, often working for upwards of ten hours a day.

*4. Traildogs feel the bone-deep satisfaction, along with aching muscles and exhaustion, from giving everything to their passion and living their values full-tilt.*
Many nights I have known the pleasure of lying down on our blow-up mattress in the tent, tired out by a day of paddling, hiking or both, and other rigors of living outdoors. Most traildogs lie down at night in far less comfortable conditions. But I imagine in the seconds before they fall into the kind of sleep that comes only from being physically spent from hours of unfathomably hard work, traildogs must glance back on all they accomplished that day, allowing themselves a humble pride in the positive difference they have made in the lives of hundreds, more likely thousands, of people who will pass this way for years to come. Surely such inner knowing must help to usher in the sweetest and deepest sleep.

*5. Traildogs sacrifice their own comfort for a greater cause.*
Traildogs forego activities and comforts that most of us enjoy regularly, such as relaxing vacations, time with friends and family, and the chance to pursue other interests. They live without a stove, kitchen sink, refrigerator, hot shower, and comfortable bed, and instead of dropping into easy chairs they sit on logs, boulders, or the ground. And they do this for months at a stretch.

Not many of us could do what they do. I know I couldn't. For many reasons, it's a status bestowed on a rare few. But at the same time, I believe we all have traildog traits or tendencies. In my life, for example, I've been the best mother I know how to be. After almost twenty-six years of service to the University of Michigan, I like to think I can look back at the legacy of work I left behind with some pride. Being married since 1977 (which has required occasional small doses of traildog-like effort) makes me feel like a traildog who got off easy. Writing and making plans to publish this book has brought out the traildog in me: hour after hour of writing, endless editing, planning, and tackling the list of tasks I must check off before I can finally hold the book in my hand.

In ending, I pay homage to the real traildogs out there, and offer a few questions for the rest of us to ask as we consider ways we can paint our lives, both within and without, in wild and crazy traildog colors.

## *Questions to Ponder*

- Where do your traildog traits show up in your life?
- Is there an interest or passion where you would like to engage more of your inner traildog, one that you may someday regret missing out on if you don't?
- If so, which comforts (or part of your comfort zone) would you need to give up to just go for it?
- What would it take for you to reach your "dog year" (your rite of passage in achieving a big goal)?
- What kinds of rewards might await you there?

CHAPTER 22

# Love the Hills

FOR MANY YEARS and counting, each year on the Friday before President's Day weekend in February, my husband and I have finished packing the car at around 6:00 a.m. and headed north on U.S. 23 to drive the 352 door-to-door miles to Stokely Creek Lodge in Goulais River, Ontario. There, we have cross-country skied for five days, eaten three filling, delicious meals a day, slept four nights with a soundness that hours of vigorous exercise during the day have virtually guaranteed, and spent time with friends, old and new, over meals and as we relaxed near well-tended fireplaces in the evenings.

One year we met Morgan (not his real name), a Brit at heart from Ontario who looked to be in his sixties but whose skiing stamina was more like a man twenty years younger. With a clever wit and sparkling eyes, Morgan was a born entertainer. Right away, I made it a point to try to remember his pithy one-liners long enough to jot them down later in my journal.

The skiing was good that year. It had been, as the manager told us with a grimace, almost too much of a banner year for snow, accumulating in an astonishing forty-eight-inch base. This much snow was tough on the aging grooming machines the Stokely mechanics managed somehow to keep running year after year with hardware akin to wire and paper clips. On the third morning, we woke to two to three inches of fresh powder. The new snow would make it a bit easier to herringbone up the hills. But it also would add drag to our glide, perhaps the most important part of cross-country skiing. (As the instructor said to me at the only skiing lesson I ever had: "Most of cross-country skiing is hard work, but not your glide. Your glide is *free*.")

Despite the promise of the better grip and glide of waxed skis, for the past twenty years or so my husband and I have stuck with wax-less ones. Perhaps, as we get older, the tantalizing promise of better grip and glide in just the right places will eventually win us over. So far, though, we haven't been willing to spend any of our precious time at Stokely bent over skis in the waxing room.

Having been cross-country skiers for more than thirty-five years, in the year we met Morgan we were enjoying our fourteenth trip (or more aptly put, pilgrimage) to our beloved Stokely Creek. That year, for the first time I found myself thinking deeply about *glide*. After cresting a hill and skiing down its other side, I stopped briefly at the bottom and turned back to look up at the hill as if I were about to climb it. As expected, it appeared much steeper to my eye than the degree of downhill I had just skied. When my husband and I ski, he typically leads the way in the tracks. I enjoy watching the easy way he skis downhill, letting gravity and momentum pull him gently, his poles hanging loosely at his sides, whereas I tend to add to my glide by planting and pushing off with either one or both of my ski poles.

That year, resentment bubbled up in me at how much smaller and more gradual the downhill skiing seemed when compared to the rigors of pushing uphill. These feelings stuck in my throat like a fishbone that refused to go down. My rational side knew they were silly bordering on stupid, but as the days went by my emotions became a nonsensical anger. One day my husband and I skied Bas' Bypass, a cutover trail that ended at the western end of the Pickard Lake Trail. (Because of its gentle ups and downs through the maple, birch, beech, pine and hemlock trees that give way in places to a view of the snow-covered lake, Pickard is one of my favorites.) But before we made the turn, I frowned, looked back over my shoulder at the Bas' Bypass, and said to Rick with a shake of my head, "That trail defies the law of physics. We climbed and then climbed some more. *Why doesn't the downhill ever arrive*?" I felt cheated and even a little outraged. With a sigh, I turned away, planted my first pole, and skied toward Pickard Lake.

That night over dinner, the conversation turned to hills and I shared my "it defies the law of physics" conclusion about Bas' Bypass. Without skipping a beat, Morgan said with a trace of a smile, "Oh, but one must love the hills, *especially* the hills," then resumed eating his salad. His words hit me like a gentle, wake-up slap on the cheek. Love the hills … *love* the hills? *You've got to be kidding*, my cynical side responded within. Off and on for the rest of the night, I turned his words over and over in my mind, like gemstones in my palm … *love the hills … love the hills.*

The next morning, I decided to try to love the hills as much as the glide, turning the phrase into a mantra as I climbed. What was there to love, I asked myself sincerely, about these hills? Over the course of a few hours, answers came to me. For one thing, climbing hills is the honest, honorable price we pay for being so deep in this hardwood forest, amidst hills that seem to wear hairdos that look, without their summer lushness, a bit like punk hairdos. The climb had my heart beating so hard that when we stopped for a moment, I heard a pulsing sound inside my head …floosh … floosh. What was the sound, the rhythm? What would I make of it? Would I turn it into anger and resentment at the need to climb? Or would I see it as the sound of blood coursing through me, as the sound of health and well-being, as the sound of being blissfully alive, as the good fortune of being one of the few people there that day, deep in these northern woods? Yes, I whispered to myself. Yes. I listened closely and heard the sweet sound.

At the peak of each hill, I gave myself to the downward pull of gravity and sweet glide. I savored it until it had almost spent itself and I once again had to push and pole, push and pole. *Love the hills.* Yes, I will. I will love the hills. I whisper into the wind, "Thank you, Morgan."

## *Questions to Ponder*

- What actions in your life remind you of skiing uphill?
- Are there hills either in your present or past that it might behoove you to learn to love? What is about them you could love?

IV

# Gratitude and Compassion

I am satisfied ... I see, dance, laugh, sing.

– Walt Whitman, *Leaves of Grass*

CHAPTER 23

# Never Sit on Your Cat

As the oldest of eight children, my father was part of a large family that gave us cousins galore, eighteen to be exact. Two of them (also girls) shared my birth year and played feature roles in some of my fondest childhood memories. My mother, though, had only one sibling, a younger brother. Unable to have children of their own, this uncle and aunt adopted a boy, Richie (short for Richard), who was also born in 1950, the same Baby Boomer year that produced me.

I looked forward excitedly to visiting Richie and his parents, which we did almost every summer. They lived in the small town of Newfield, New York, thirteen miles southeast of Ithaca, where my uncle was a professor of agricultural economics at Cornell University. (After serving in the navy, he completed his undergraduate degree on the G.I. Bill, stayed on to earn his doctorate, and then joined the faculty—all at Cornell.) In contrast, my father, who had hungered to be a civil engineer, worked in a machine shop all his life. Consequently, our two families had vastly different incomes and understandably different lifestyles. My uncle and aunt owned a large colonial home on Main Street, west of downtown, with a backyard that sloped gently down to a small stream. Because their home and everything in it—from dishes on the table, to art on the wall, to furniture–was so much nicer than ours, without envy (being just a kid), I saw them as being rich.

In our family archive is a rare family photo of my three brothers, my parents, and me standing on the front porch during a summer visit a few years before Mom died. In the photo, I'm five years old and rail-thin with sun-bleached hair. My mother is in her favorite place, under my father's arm. She was a good seven inches shorter than Dad, who stood at just over six feet. I love the carefree feeling in her eyes. I stand a bit off to the right, squinting from the sun and smiling the kid's easy smile that comes when all feels well in the world.

Earlier that afternoon, while our families were walking in downtown Newfield, we came across a woman with a box of mewing kittens to give away. My cousin and I immediately began to jump up and down, begging our parents, "Please, please, please!" Eventually giving in, our parents let each of us pick one to bring home. Back at the house, my cousin and I sat on the sidewalk in front, thrilled to be holding our kittens. Excitement played over my cousin's face as he suggested we play Follow the Leader with our kitties. Always willing to go along, I enthusiastically agreed. My cousin took the lead. He put his cat above his head. I did the same. He put his cat in the grass and let him take a few steps. I followed. Then he blurted, "Sit on your cat," and pretended to sit on his. I, however, didn't pretend. I did as I was told, and followed the leader.

A moment later, when I held the poor creature out in front of me, its mouth made a horrible yawning motion that was clearly not a yawn. In an instant, my horrible mistake hit me hard. I rushed into the house, calling, "Daddy! Daddy!" But within the hour my new kitty was dead. (I'm quite sure my uncle or my father, seeing that the cat was in pain and unable to recover, drowned her in a pail in the backyard to put her out of her misery). We buried her under a tree and held a short funeral. My heart was broken. Since that day, there has never been another kitten or cat to take her place.

What lessons did I take from this childhood mistake?

1. The first and absurdly obvious lesson is never to sit on a cat or on any other living creature not equipped to bear weight. But even at that young age, I knew, of course, it was wrong to sit on my cat. So why did I do it anyway? Looking back, I believe I got caught up in the excitement of the moment. Plus, I loved and trusted my cousin.
2. The second lesson is how important it is to understand and forgive the innocent if foolish decisions children sometimes make. Since

the executive function of the brain isn't fully developed until sometime between the ages of twenty and twenty-nine, which is one of the reasons why college students engage in so many risky behaviors, my inability, in that split second, to interrupt a terrible decision had physiological roots. Simply put, my brain was too young. Looking back, I'm glad I never blamed my cousin (whose death in a terrible car crash when he in his twenties broke my heart) for what happened that day with our kittens. (Perhaps my brain, thankfully, was too young for that, too.)

3. The third and final lesson I took from this painful childhood experience is that although Follow the Leader is a childhood game, as we mature it's a game with a darker side we can continue to play, sometimes unconsciously. Naivety—a trait I continue to manifest at times—can be beneficial in its tendency to keep the mind open. But without sufficient caution, it can be dangerous. Before following, I learned that day and from reflecting many times on this sad experience, *stop*. Listen to your inner conscience and trust its wisdom. This kind of lesson can take a lifetime to truly embrace, and I confess I'm still working on it.

Perhaps you can use my sad story to take a small step closer to the powerful, authentic place of inner wisdom that's ever present in each of us, especially at times when we pause before we act to truly think about what we plan to do and the likely results.

## *Questions to Ponder*

- Are there ways you have played Follow the Leader in life without intending to? Do you have regrets about it?
- Are there any painful but innocent childhood incidents that you need to forgive yourself for?

## CHAPTER 24

# Give Your Parents a Break

My father and mother fell in love when they were in high school when Dad was a senior, Mom a year behind him. As a kid, I asked Dad once how the two of them fell in love. He said it happened on a day in June when he walked past her house on the main street of Groton, Vermont, which, it being a small town, he had done hundreds, if not thousands, of times before.

There on the porch, my mother-to-be Dorothy was sitting in a chair, hulling a large bowl of strawberries. Something about how she looked at him pulled him to stop, he told me, to say hello. Soon he was sitting on the top step with his back against a post, talking with her as she worked. As he told me the story, his eyes gazed into the distance. "There was just something about the way your mother smelled that day, sitting on the porch, her fingers stained with strawberry juice," he said. Their time together that afternoon kindled a love that grew quickly and bound them together from that point on.

They married in the fall of 1934, shortly after my mother finished her first and only year of "normal school," which at that time trained young women to be teachers. My mother's mother and stepfather (Grammie and Grampa Parker) were terribly upset that my mother had dropped out of school to marry this man from a large, poor family who had no money or prospects. To them, education was vital.

Sewell Carpenter, my mother's father, who died when Mom was just shy of five years old, was a postmaster and at one time owned a bicycle shop. Although almost no stories have come down to us about Grampa Sewell, Louise (his wife and our grandmother) clearly believed in the value of education. Plus, Ernest Parker, who married Grammie after she lost Sewell in 1920 to the flu pandemic, worked for many years as a quarryman in a granite quarry, and later as a stonecutter in a granite shed. As a laborer in an industry that may well have contributed to his premature death from tuberculosis, he, too, would almost certainly have appreciated the value of a good education. Having wanted desperately to attend college, my father agreed wholeheartedly with my grandparents. He, too, urged Dorothy to continue her studies, but she would have none of it. The possibility of losing my father to another woman while she was at school was simply too much for her to bear.

After marrying, my mother ached to have children, but it would be seven long years before she gave birth to their first child. During those childless years, she watched sisters-in-law and friends bring their babies home from the hospital. Although I'm sure she put on a good face when she paid a social visit after each of these births, family lore has it that upon returning home my mother would sit and cry. (If there was an explanation for my parents' initial difficulty getting pregnant, it never came to light.) Finally, in 1941, my oldest brother Brent was born, followed less than two years later by another son, Brian, and then, after a gap of almost six years, another boy, Peter. Financially and otherwise, it would have made good sense for them to stop having kids after Peter was born. Nevertheless, my mother convinced my father to try one more time for a girl. In early November 1950, when the nurse laid my swaddled body into my mother's eager arms, my lucky mix of X and Y chromosomes brought her much-yearned-for dream to life.

I deeply loved my father, who died in 1983 when I was only thirty-three, and remember him as a wonderful dad. He was good-natured, patient, calm, supportive, and understanding. He was also hardworking, a man who faced challenges big and small with a steady hand. Dad was also friendly and well liked. One time when I asked him why so many people liked him, he thought for a moment and said, "Well, probably because I like them."

On the other hand, Dad could be exacting. One of my brothers remembers building a structure from Tinker Toys. When he brought it to our father to show him what he had done (proudly, I expect), Dad studied it for a few minutes and then offered advice disguised in the form of a question something like, "If you put these pieces here, do you think it could be even better?"

Although I'm sure Dad meant well, to this day my brother remembers the frustration of having come up a little short.

In my early twenties on a visit home, I sat at the dining room table with a monthly checking statement in hand, furious with the bank for having recently charged me a fee for a bounced check. To this day, I remember Dad asking, "Do you mean you've never balanced your checkbook after receiving a bank statement?" We all know what my sheepish answer was. At times my father had a way of making us feel not quite good enough, albeit in his mild-mannered, non-confrontational way. (I should add that one of my brothers distinctly remembers that it was he—not our father—who had the checking account conversation with me. But since the memory tucked firmly in my brain is of having it with Dad, I've decided to stay with my version of the story despite how unreliable human memories tend to be.)

Another rather mysterious characteristic of Dad's was his tendency to withhold compliments or praise. I'm sure he was proud of our accomplishments. All four of us were good kids; we did well in school and stayed out of trouble. Our oldest brother, for example, was and is the proverbial first-born high achiever. But despite Dad's pride in us, it bears asking, "What made him so sparing with his praise?"

When I learned about the work of Dr. Carol Dweck, a Stanford University professor and researcher and the author of the book *Mindset*, which I recommend highly, I felt sure I had picked up at least one piece of this puzzle. Through research, Dr. Dweck and other social scientists have revealed that praise can have has a dark side when it sends a message of conditional love. Be "good" and you'll earn the stamp of approval. It turns out that riding shotgun next to the good feelings praise tends to deliver is the ever-present threat that *next time* we might screw up or do something stupid. This sense of fear tends to squash what Dr. Dweck calls a "growth mindset," which puts the focus on learning and growing instead of on achievement and success. (Dweck, 6-7). Although it's true Dad didn't praise us, even when we deserved it, neither did he dish up scorn, even when we made idiotic mistakes.

During the summer after I finished high school, Peter, the brother closest to me in age, was back home after a riotously fun first year of college, with lousy grades to match. My brother had landed a summer job in the same machine shop where Dad had taken a job a quarter of a century earlier as his ticket to a regular paycheck and access to good public education for his children. To this man who had, as a young man, ached to study engineering, his intention for each of his kids to earn a college education was not up for debate. The question wasn't *whether* my brothers and I would attend college; the only question was *where.*

My brother Peter, twenty years old at the time, engaged in the usual shenanigans of the day, which included bouts of drinking with friends. Three years after my mother died of cancer in 1959, Dad married a woman he met at church. At that same time, Dad sold the house he had built in North Springfield for my mother (and for our whole family), paid off some of Mom's medical bills, and moved the three of us into our stepmother's small, three-bedroom ranch on the south side of Springfield, just a few miles away. (My two older brothers were away at college.)

One morning when Dad opened the blinds in the living room of our stepmother's house, he met with quite a surprise—the sight of my brother, stretched out in the middle of the front lawn, sound asleep. Earlier that morning, my brother's friends had dropped him there. South Street, where we lived, saw a fair amount of traffic by Vermont standards. So even at that early hour, a steady stream of cars passed by the house. Surely at least a few of those drivers must have puzzled over this young man lying on our front lawn.

So, what did my father do after seeing my brother? Another kind of father might have justifiably stormed outside to yell, "Get your sorry rear end up this minute and take it into the house! You are an embarrassment to the entire family," but not Dad. He quietly opened the door, walked calmly to where my brother lay, bent down to give his shoulder a nudge, and said, "Time to get up, son. You need to get ready for work." Which is exactly what my brother did. To my knowledge–and our father's credit–Dad never mentioned it again.

A couple of years later, it was my turn to arrive home in a stupor. Inebriated and unsteady on my feet, I knew there was no way, even in our small house, that I could stumble to my bedroom and back out to the kitchen to turn out the small light tucked under one of the kitchen cupboards that, with its glow, signaled to my parents that at least one of us, my brother or me, hadn't made it home yet. So, taking my chances to go directly to my bedroom without a return kitchen visit, I switched off the light and then slowly, gingerly walked as quietly as possible through the small dining room, past the table and chairs on my right and the matching china-filled buffet on my left. When I reached the hallway, I let out an audible sigh. With only a few short steps to my bedroom, I thought I was home free.

Suddenly, the overhead hall light blazed on, as I shielded my eyes. There, less than a foot in front of me stood my father in his pajamas. *Busted* I thought to myself. I smiled stupidly, swayed a little, slurred the words "Hi, Dad," walked into my room and quietly closed the door. The next day my stepmother carried on about how irresponsible I was, but not one word from Dad. His willingness to let us experience our dopey behavior and mistakes without getting angry and verbally beating us up about it was, I believe, a great gift.

At the same time, in considering Dr. Dweck and the notion of mindset, might Dad have been doing us a favor by not linking our value or his love to our accomplishments or achievements? My guess is that like most parents back then, Dad never gave much thought to a philosophy of parenting. Instead, he probably took life one day at a time, hoping, I imagine, that through his example we kids would inherit his sense of integrity and responsibility. (I must pause to add that he and one of his sisters [from a family of eight kids] had the good fortune to be sent to live for a few years with their grandparents [on their mother's side]. While living there, they were exposed to a highly functioning household quite different from what they were used to at home, where money was often scarce, the family's domicile, never permanent, generally left much to be desired, and where far too often their father came home "full of drink." In reflecting on the kind of father Dad turned out to be, I'm sure my brothers and I owe these great-grandparents many thanks.)

Through Dad's unspoken unconditional love, coupled with patience and silence in the face of stupidity, as well as actions and words, he steadily conveyed a great deal of trust in our ability to "make it through." Which is just what we did, over time, each of us in our own way.

*Postscript.* Because my brother Peter generously allowed me to include a potentially embarrassing story about him, I must tell you that he went on to do well in all areas of his life—as a father, a husband, a student, a professional, and in many other roles. That kid who passed out drunk on the front lawn? He's one of the finest people and nicest guys you could meet.

## *Questions to Ponder*

- Just like my father, no parent or caregiver is perfect. Within that context, what were the greatest gifts you received from your parents or caregivers?
- As adults, often the messages we heard from our parents (or the things we most needed to hear that they didn't say) continue to play in our minds (or be painfully absent). If you were to claim the power to "parent" yourself, what's the most important message you would send to yourself?

CHAPTER 25

# Lessons from a Broken Tooth

One Friday evening years ago, I was about to turn in for the night. Although I usually floss my teeth in front of the bathroom mirror, that night I did a lazier version as I stood next to the bureau in our bedroom. Then, a sudden shock–the space that had held one of my front teeth was now, my tongue told me, quite empty. Looking down, my concern became more real. There, indeed, on the carpet near my feet sat a part of my tooth, which I quickly bent down to pick up. I later learned it was a lateral incisor, the one located on the right side of the mouth, between the central incisor (aka big tooth) and the canine. It didn't so much break as shear off, leaving a ragged and unsightly stump.

When I walked into the bathroom to take a closer look, I was aghast by the changed, decidedly not-improved me staring back from the mirror. The remaining bit of tooth was an ugly brown (a result, my dentist would remind me later, of an earlier root canal, which means the tooth was quite dead.) With its jagged edges, it looked rotten. I was astonished by how much this one bad tooth had suddenly, sickeningly affected my appearance, and my ability to smile confidently.

The first lesson of this experience washed over me just minutes after the tooth broke off. Despite how awful I looked, my prevalent feeling was gratitude. *Where was I?* At home. *What was I doing?* Getting ready for bed. *When was it?* A Friday night with no big plans for the weekend. *Who was I with?* My husband, who would love me no matter how I looked. Other embarrassing scenarios jumped to mind of when the tooth might have otherwise decided to break: while having lunch with a friend, giving a presentation, or meeting new people at a networking event. That night I climbed into bed not glad that my tooth had broken, but feeling lucky indeed about when and where it had happened.

The following morning, I called my dentist's office to leave a message with the answering service. Not five minutes later, my dentist called back. This dentist who, along with his capable, friendly staff, has taken good care of our family's teeth since our move to Ann Arbor thirty years ago, is also a friend.

Over the weekend I lay low, talking almost ventriloquist-like, and when I needed to talk, hiding the right side of my mouth with a few fingers. Then, on Monday, my dentist kindly squeezed me into his schedule. I was relieved to learn the tooth was in better shape than it first appeared. Although my dentist needed to insert a titanium post to help secure the crown that he would place on top of it, thankfully I didn't require a tooth implant, which, based on what I've heard from a few friends, includes living for weeks without the tooth, and costs as much as, among other things, a high-end vacation. Not quite two hours later, I left the dentist office wearing a temporary crown, reveling in the pleasure of once again feeling free to smile.

This experience took me back to when I was in elementary school. During the years between my mother's cancer diagnosis and the day she died, dental care for us kids was the last thing on my father's mind—far, far behind his need to work full time, keep the household running, watch helplessly as medical bills piled up, and see the love of his life slowly waste away. On top of this, my brothers and I ate more than our share of candy and probably brushed our teeth once a day, if that, and probably not well. Over those years, bacteria and plaque on our teeth led inevitably to cavities, lots of them.

A year or so after my mother died, my father decided something *had* to be done about our teeth. So, he made some sort of payment arrangement with a hometown dentist, launching a long series of visits to his office. I still remember the dentist's treatment room vividly: the tall ceiling, the dull green walls, the chair covered in worn black leather, the two-piece headrest I leaned my head back into, the small round sink next to the chair with its small, unceasing sound of water flushing away spit and whatever else was in it.

I dreaded trips to that office. Plus, I found our dentist to be a grouchy old man with a stern, scolding look. One day in school I called my father at work (which, Dad had made perfectly clear, was something we were allowed to do only in an emergency) to beg him not to make me go to the dentist that afternoon. Knowing that a good day to go to the dentist never comes, he wisely insisted that I go ahead with the appointment. Looking back on all this, I'm deeply thankful to him for sticking to the plan despite my piteous pleas. Heaven knows how he managed to pay for our dental care. In hindsight, I also appreciate the dentist for his willingness to take us on as patients, allowing our father to pay him over time. Hidden somewhere beneath his grumpy, scary exterior was a vein of goodness, and probably another one of kindness.

Because of those early years of bad dental care, and in spite of those many visits to our dentist, I have since needed a great deal of dental work. As to just how many crowns are in my mouth, I've lost track, something like twelve or thirteen. Truthfully, I've done my share of complaining about the cost of all this work. At one point, I started grumbling that my mouth was worth more than my car, and this may be true even in today's dollars.

But on the Monday morning after my front tooth broke, when the receptionist told me what the charges were, as I wrote in the rather sizable amount on the check, my only feeling was one of deep gratitude. Staring at that dreadful-looking tooth for three days had turned my head around to a new appreciation for investments over the years in costly dental work. How might my life have been different without the benefits of a pleasant-looking, self-confident smile. Without dental care, I may well have also experienced the social stigmas commonly held against people with visibly bad teeth, and quite possibly negative effects on my overall health. I also thought about our daughters and how different their lives might have unfolded if they hadn't had good dental care, including braces.

After our younger daughter's mature teeth came in, they were such a jumbled mess that for a school assignment in elementary school she wrote a parody about a girl whose crooked teeth traumatized everyone who set eyes on her. Somewhere we still have the article, which includes a snapshot of her taken in a moment when she covered her eyes and flashed a big grin that revealed those crazy teeth in all their glory. If we hadn't been able to afford braces for her, I believe that mouthful of drastically crooked teeth would have cast a shadow on her sense of self and also on some of her life decisions and experiences.

Being able to comfortably pay for a new crown on my broken tooth—and for all the dental work I had paid for over the years—has given me immeasurably more than healthy teeth. So, if you ever catch me complaining about how much I have paid my dentists over the years, shoot me a look that reminds me of the challenges my father overcame to secure the early dental care he insisted on and for my husband's and my ability over the years to invest in healthy, attractive teeth for our daughters and for ourselves.

## *Questions to Ponder*

- What kind of difficult experiences have you endured that you were later thankful for?
- What's one thing you tend to forget to be grateful for? How might you change that?

CHAPTER 26

# Forgive—Especially When It's Hard

July 1961. My stepmother walked into the house after her honeymoon trip with my father to attend a church conference in Troy, New York. Excited to have my father and new mom back home, I rushed up to her to ask if she could sew another new outfit for my Barbie doll (just one of the kindnesses she showered on me on my special visits to her house). "Maybe a blue dress this time? Would you?"

Standing uncomfortably close to me in her small kitchen, she delivered news that felt, looking back on it, like a bucket of ice water tossed in my face. Gripping my thin arm in her fingers, she spoke slowly enough to be sure her words hit their mark squarely: "Surely, you don't think things are going to be the same now that your father and I are married?" It was not a question. The attention she had showered on me while courting my father, the very thing I had hungered for most since Mom died, and, honestly, long before that, as the cancer had steadily eroded her body and mind in the months before she died, suddenly the attention I needed so badly, and had relished for a short time, came to a screeching halt.

This incident would prove to be only the first of a stretched-out line of hurts my stepmother would pierce me with between that day in the kitchen and seven years later when, only two days after graduating from high school, I would escape with my best friend to the shores of the Atlantic in Ogunquit, Maine, into the first delicious days of my independence.

Although my stepmother has been dead for many years, to this day I carry hurtful memories. But rather than giving me the satisfaction I desired, over time I realized that my frequent retelling of tales about her emotionally abusive behavior only reopened old wounds. "See how I have suffered," the stories said. "See how I survived. See this awful person who has hurt me, and, by contrast, see how much better of a person I am because I would never be like her." In truth those stories were like bricks carried in a worn backpack, one I refused to put down despite its straps digging into my skin and lugging around a burden that only held me back. As if the titles of these stories were affixed to gateposts new friends were required enter through, I told my "mean stepmother" stories again and again. (Believe me, you don't want to hear them.) Now, after more than fifty years, I ask myself: "Will I ever be able to let these stories and hurts slip into the past where they belong, and, at long last, leave them there?"

For this kind of martyr-like behavior, other names and metaphors work just as well: grudges, old anger, grievances, bad blood, bitterness, resentment, bones to pick. The point is that when we refuse to forgive those who, as we see it, have trespassed against us, *we* carry the bricks, *we* drag the chains, *and we weigh ourselves down*. By harboring grudges against people, in a warped way we bind them to us more tightly.

The answer is yes. I am ready. Let these words be a vow to the world that I am done with these stories. Enough. But since forgiveness, especially for still-hurtful grievances, is neither easy nor simple, it can be helpful to move, step-by-step, through a process that takes into account how complicated and highly emotional forgiveness can be. What follows is a process that has worked well for me and that I hope may be useful to you.

*1. Get clear about the nature of forgiveness, what it is and what it isn't.*

Dictionaries define *forgiveness* in these terms: to pardon, excuse, absolve, to stop feeling angry, to stop blaming. Forgiveness, though, is *not* the same as giving in, as accepting or endorsing the person's choices and behavior. Will my stepmother's treatment of me ever be acceptable or appropriate? Absolutely not. But at the same time, *I can choose* to stop blaming her for whatever unhappiness I experience today. After all, she's been dead for more than twenty years. Since her death (and much earlier than that), who has been in charge of my life? Right. That would be me.

As I see it, forgiveness is a form of exercise for our "response-ability" muscles. Although we sometimes have little or no control over what happens to us, we have a great deal of say over how we respond, especially as adults.

*2. Forgive for* you.
A cardinal rule of forgiveness is to do it primarily for *you* and for *your* benefit as an act of loving *yourself.* What are the benefits of forgiveness to *you*? For one thing, through forgiveness you can stop viewing (and treating) yourself like a victim and, in this way, reclaim some of your personal power. Next, you can lighten your emotional load. Finally, you can forgive *others* to strengthen your ability to forgive *yourself* for your own inevitable missteps.

*3. Make a vow to stop telling your victim stories and stick to it.*
Where would people be without stories? Stories enrich us, and our lives, in countless ways. Some stories, though, keep us stuck in negative mental and emotional ruts, like continuing to drive down the same dark road where disaster waits. When we keep our victim stories alive, we only deepen the ruts in the road and the pain inside ourselves.

*4. Shift your label of the person who has wronged you from villain to complex human being, and then, from this new perspective, try to look at him or her with a kinder spirit.*
Over her lifetime, my stepmother made many friends. She also did many good deeds. Immediately inside the doors of the church where her memorial service took place hung a beautifully framed lace "painting" of the Last Supper that she painstakingly tatted (a largely lost needlework art), and donated to the church. It is a work of art. At her service, the church pews held more friends than one would expect of a person who had lived into her nineties. Many of her friends wept, deeply grieved by her death. Clearly, my stepmother had many sides, some of which I had adamantly refused to look for or acknowledge.

To begin with, my stepmother made enormous personal sacrifices when she married Dad. After living comfortably in a small three-bedroom ranch house for many years, she gave up a great deal of privacy by making room for my father and my brother Peter and me, exposing herself to the vagaries of three other human beings living in close quarters and bringing into her tranquil home two kids racing full speed into adolescence, the time of life all parents dread but, for my stepmother, without the benefit and sustenance of happy memories from younger years. Suddenly, she was also cooking for *four* people instead of one. When I imagine myself stepping into her shoes at that time, I see how big and difficult a transition it must have been for her. Yes, the circumstances were tough for me, but they were no piece of cake for her, either.

My stepmother also improved my father's life in all sorts of ways. Moving into her home allowed him to sell the house he had built and subsequently pay off some of the towering stack of unpaid medical bills from mother's illness and funeral services. My stepmother also lifted from his shoulders the sole responsibility of keeping a household together while working fulltime. She gave him daily companionship and–surely–intimacy, which, at the age of forty-seven, my father must have both needed and yearned for.

She also offered him a social life and more fun. (For years, they were regular square dancers, wearing a collection of brightly colored clothing that my stepmother, a highly skilled seamstress, made for them: detailed cowboy shirts for my father and full, petticoat skirts or dresses for her.) Without a doubt, she loved my father, and when I let go of telling my "stepmother stories," it was much easier to see and appreciate the many ways their marriage was good for Dad.

In fairness, I must also say that based on the stories I heard from my stepmother about her growing up years, her childhood and early years were far from easy. Her father, a strict, unforgiving man, struck out physically at times, without warning, when he became angry. Later she also had the courage to leave an early-in-life, unhappy marriage and subsequently find a way to support herself and her two young children. (Her first child was born ten years earlier than my oldest brother. So, her son and daughter, who became my stepbrother and stepsister, were nineteen and fifteen years older than I was, respectively [almost a full generation], and their children [my stepmother's grandchildren] were young enough to feel, to me, like kids.) Yes, like everyone else, my stepmother was a complex person, and, furthermore, a person who faced life challenges with no small measure of courage and fierce determination.

*5. Choose or create a ritual for letting go of your grievance, and then use it.* Many rituals, practices, and exercises exist to help us engage actively in forgiving others. Our task is to find one that works.

I'll offer a few examples I've learned about over the years.

- Write some words on a piece of paper or choose a small object that captures the hurtful incident, and then burn the piece of paper or bury the object.
- Write a forgiveness contract in which you firmly commit to completely forgiving and releasing the person who has "wronged" you. Share this contract with someone you trust.
- (If applicable) Seek spiritual support or guidance in letting go.
- Unleash your creativity and make up your own ritual.

My forgiveness ritual of choice is a practice called loving-kindness meditation, which is easy to learn, flexible, and simple to do. In tune with the nature of forgiveness, in a loving-kindness meditation practice, the first step is to send loving-kindness to oneself, only then moving on to other people, and then moving, by stages, from people you love, to people for whom your feelings are positive but largely neutral, and only then to people you perceive as being in the wrong.

Below are the loving-kindness words I use currently (they seem to change over time):

May [the person's name] be filled with loving-kindness.
May [he/she] be safe and protected.
May [he/she] be healthy and strong.
May [he/she] be happy and at ease.

The tangibility and power of ritual, including loving-kindness meditation, can be instrumental in the *practice* of forgiveness.

Before ending, I offer you two more thoughts. First, it is *never* too late to forgive. In fact, forgiving a long-standing hurt may be one of the best things you ever do for yourself. Finally, forgive often and generously. Forgive the driver who cuts you off. Forgive your friend for forgetting your birthday. Forgive your stepmother for having been the wounded, imperfect person she was. Most of all, forgive *you* for the foibles and missteps that come with being human. Give *yourself* the gift of forgiveness today and every day.

I end this chapter by saying publicly to my stepmother: *May you be filled with loving-kindness. May you be safe and protected. May you be healthy and strong. May you be happy and at ease.* And yes, finally: *I forgive you.*

## *Questions to Ponder*

- Can you think of a way in which refusing to forgive someone is hurting only (or mostly) you?
- Is there a hurtful story, one that may be keeping you stuck in the past, that you're ready to stop telling?
- As you think of a person whom you're having a hard time forgiving, what's at least one positive attribute about that person other people have admired or appreciated?
- What type of forgiveness ritual might work best for you?

CHAPTER 27

# Bring Home *Real* Treasures from Vacation

*Say ya to da U.P., eh!* This popular bumper sticker, written in the dialect of native "Yoopers" (residents of Michigan's Upper Peninsula), parodies the "Say YES to Michigan" campaign that the state's department of tourism ran during the late 1980s. Using this dialect, with its Scandinavian and French-Canadian roots, I begin this chapter by saying to you, "Dis summer my husband and I said a big ya to da U.P." Our trip consisted of three nights staying in a remote cabin between Munising and Grand Marais.

Afterward, as we drove south on I-75 toward Ann Arbor, we gassed up at a station outside Mackinaw City where restrooms were only available in the adjacent gift shop. On my walk to the women's room, I passed display after display of gaudy souvenirs from which I couldn't escape fast enough. After we climbed back into the car, to help erase the image of those awful souvenirs I decided to take stock of the *real treasures* we were bringing home with us.

*1. The power of big waves on Lake Superior*

The first treasure on my list came to us while we hiked the Mosquito Falls trail in Pictured Rocks National Lakeshore, which we have visited several times but can never get enough of. A good ten minutes before we reached a short bluff overlooking the frigid but beckoning Lake Superior, we heard waves slam into shore in quick succession.

By no means, though, were large waves on Lake Superior new to us. While the girls were growing up, every other year or so we stuffed our station wagon and utility trailer with enough camping gear, food, and equipment to let us live outdoors for a week, and then pointed our caravan north toward Lake Superior Provincial Park. A six-hour drive from Ann Arbor, this 384,610-acre park offers so many beaches, hiking trails, and smaller inland lakes that it's tough to choose among them when making plans for the day. Over the years, our visits to the lake the Ojibwa native Americans called *Gichigami* (big sea), which morphed into the modern day Gitche Gumee, included days of winds so strong they pushed the water into white-capped waves that crashed relentlessly onto the beach.

But despite our many earlier experiences, that day on the big lake was different. Never before had we seen Superior's waves that tall or powerful. They were like ancient gods thundering to shore. Walking around the bend, we sat on a log in a spot that tempered the strong winds out of the northwest. In awe, we watched the waves crash against the shore and then into each other, coming and going. Further down the shore, in the next inlet, the spray from the crashing waves was as tall as the cliff. Without a doubt, this experience was true treasure for us to bring home, special new memories of this big water, its enormous waves and the power in beholding such majesty.

*2. Hundreds of dollars on the walls and much more*

Our next treasure was lunch at the Bear Trap Inn that sits a quarter mile east of the Melstrand General Store. Since the Bear Trap was on our way into town, we passed it at least twice each day. Despite a large printed sign that spelled OPEN in fat black letters on a white background that sat in the window at all hours of the day or night, we learned to trust only the bright orange neon sign hanging near the front door. Locals had told us that along with the West Bay Diner in Grand Marais, the Bear Trap serves the best food around. So, on a heavily overcast day in the middle of our stay, we stopped there for lunch. In addition to enjoying the restaurant's laid-back, down-home atmosphere and good food, our stop there delivered up new treasures well worth bringing home.

Minutes after a member of the wait staff showed us to a booth, loud peals of thunder hit with almost no space between them as a storm raced our way. Suddenly the skies burst open with a pounding, heavy rain. Through the window next to our table, we watched a handful of drenched bikers in black leather and red kerchiefs quickly park their bikes and rush for the door. Dripping wet, helmets in hand, they trudged into the dining room.

Trying not to stare, I watched them out of the corner of my eye. When their food was served, one of the men, impatient with how slowly the pepper was coming out of its shaker, unscrewed the top and liberally coated his food with enough pepper to last most people for a year. As a person who is super sensitive to spicy foods, including pepper, when I saw him do this I almost choked. To my surprise, his fellow bikers were unfazed. I said quietly to my husband that he was either out to prove his masculinity beyond a shred of doubt, or had simply killed his taste buds over time.

Another treasure at the Bear Claw came in the form of messages written on dollar bills. Hundreds, if not thousands, of them were tacked to every visible wall. Some bills were also affixed to the ceiling, where they sat like wisps of hair on a comb-over. Each dollar carried a unique, handwritten message. *Cynthia and Bruce Forever* was written on one of the bills next to us, on another, the single word *BE*. A hand-drawn rough map of Michigan with a meandering line from south to north marking the route a young woman and her grandfather had hiked was tacked on the wall next to my husband. Each dollar, with its own story, had been left behind as a mark.

When I asked our waitress about the dollars, she told us it all began seven years earlier when two parties of snowmobilers who planned to take different routes wagered a bet on how long it would take them to get to the restaurant. Perhaps because they were considered to be the underdogs in the bet, the winning group wrote "time to eat some crow" on a dollar bill and tacked it to the wall for their friends to read when they arrived. On that day, our waitress said, the whole dollar bill thing took off. I loved being surrounded by those messages, like presences left behind, and the surprisingly warm connection I felt with the people who had left them there, on a medium often referred to as cold, hard cash. Treasure indeed.

*3. Mike and friends*

The greatest treasure of all from our U.P. trip arrived as if delivered in a large gift bag that, when opened, revealed several prettily wrapped packages tucked inside, delivered to us from a man I'll call Mike.

On our first full day of vacation, we paddled to Grand Island National Recreation Area from the small beach next to the Williams Landing ferry that carries people and bicycles back and forth to the island. After our return paddle, as Rick pulled the car up next to the boats, I pointed out, with a sigh, that the right front tire was almost completely flat. Long story short, we called AAA (the American Automotive Association), where a friendly, bend-over-backwards-to-help woman told us Mike had added us to his schedule and would be there within a couple of hours. A couple of hours! Hearing that news, I gave off another big sigh.

Impatient with the long wait, my husband decided to jack up the car and put on the temporary tire. As luck would have it, this tire, too, had almost no air in it. With my third sigh, I mentally added an item to our vacation prep list: be sure the spare tire is filled with air. In a matter of seconds, on the short drive to town, the typically undersized temporary tire separated from the rim. Having slowed the car to less than ten miles per hour, my husband drove the rest of the way into town with the smell of burning rubber and a great deal of loud clunking. After an agonizing few minutes, the car limped into the first gas station we saw.

Within minutes, a man from Mike's crew I'll call Sam drove up next to us in a black car whose better days were far behind it. Based on our previous, super-professional experience with AAA service, we had been expecting a big tow truck and a burly driver with an impressive collection of tools on board. But here, in Munising, the only thing this man seemed to have in tow was his girlfriend in the front seat, both of them appearing to be well into middle age.

While he stayed seated in his car next to us, we told him the story. Putting his car into gear, he said, "I'll be right back," and drove off. Within five minutes he and his friendly girlfriend were back with a tire repair kit from another nearby gas station. He climbed out of his car, removed the tire, plugged the hole, tossed it in his trunk, drove it back to the other gas station to fill it with air, and finally returned to put back on the now-plugged tire. When I asked him about the cost of the plug kit, he just shrugged. Only after I insisted did he tell me the price ($3.17). Despite his it-doesn't-matter stance, I gave him the money anyway.

At that point, Mike pulled up in his tow truck. We learned eventually that he owned an auto repair and towing shop outside Munising. His place is one of a handful of businesses clustered around an intersection of two well-traveled roads that survive on trade from townspeople but even more from the steady stream of cars on the highway. The first thing anyone would notice about Mike is his large size. He wore baggy sweatpants that must have been a multiple X size; an oversized, well-worn black work shirt; and boots that looked at least as big as my husband's size fifteens but a whole lot wider and untied. But within minutes, his more noteworthy traits emerged. I quickly came to see him as smart and friendly with a super-sized heart that thumped away in his barrel chest. His honest face and wide smile drew me in, making me instantly delighted to meet him. I loved this guy, so comfortable and at home in his big skin.

Even though our tire had been temporarily plugged and was full of air, it was in bad shape, Mike told us. He went on to say he was quite sure he had a used tire in the size we needed (he did). It being Sunday, he added, the soonest he could put on another tire would be the following morning. As this meant my husband and I would need to drive the car, on the plugged tire, back to where we were staying, he made me promise to call him when we reached our cabin so he would know we made it back okay. I agreed to do so, but then he forcefully extracted another *promise* from us (a word he enunciated), to call him in the morning *before* we drove down to his shop, so he could be on the lookout for us. Throughout the conversation, I was thinking what a treasure it was to find a guy like Mike, out here on a Sunday, helping folks like us.

Before leaving, I tipped Sam, the guy in the dilapidated black car, for bringing the tire plug kit. His eyes widened in surprise as he looked at the cash. Then he shrugged again, said thanks, and put the money in his pocket. A few minutes earlier, his girlfriend had mentioned that they never pass anyone on the side of the road without stopping to see if they need help. Clearly, these are not the kind of folks who only help others when on the clock., but the kind who lend a helping hand wherever they can. She also told me that they used to live on the west side of the lower peninsula and added emphatically that they would *never* go back. She, too, was a treasure.

The next afternoon at Mike's shop, a different employee put the used tire on our car that would hopefully get us home to Ann Arbor (it did). He was a rail-thin, young man missing a few top teeth. He wore a worn T-shirt, jeans, and on his feet, high-top, bright turquoise sneakers that looked both perfect and out of place. Quick and efficient, he was soon finished, after which we headed inside to pay.

In sharp contrast to my expectations (and a stereotype that justifiably made me ashamed of myself), when we opened the door to Mike's shop we found everything within to be orderly and clean, including the restroom. At the back of the shop, Mike stood behind an upright desk. Expecting only to hand over our credit card and sign the receipt, we learned that's not how things were done there. More "treasure," it seemed, was on the way.

The first was a story about why Mike was so delayed in getting to us the afternoon before. He'd been out on Rohdy Creek Truck Trail (known to local folks, for obvious reasons, as "rowdy road"). Later, while studying the road map, we found this road to be marked as *primitive* and *difficult to navigate*.

Turning back the clock to the previous day, Mike related how the sheriff's office called him to say a guy had called them umpteen times and would he *please* go get those people out of there so they would stop calling, for heaven's sake. So, Mike called the stranded motorist and proceeded to ask, "Are you near the Coke can or the Pepsi can?"

Here was this guy, who, Mike learned later, was not just an ill-informed tourist but also a doctor, stuck in the middle of nowhere. Without question, he had heeded the voice of his expensive car's GPS system when it instructed him in a monotone to turn south onto Rohdy Creek Truck Trail. At the time of the phone call, Mike heard the guy's wife in the background, sputtering in disgust, reminding her husband she had told him vehemently *not* to go down this road and that he would most certainly *not* be getting back into the car with all that mud on his pants and shoes. As Mike told the story, I imagined the doctor saying to himself *and now this tow truck guy at the other end of the line is asking me some crazy question about a pop can? I'm a doctor. I save lives. How did I get myself into this mess?*

Forcing himself to look around as he had been told, the doctor spied a Coke can on a nearby stump, at which point I expect his eyes and mouth opened wide. No doubt wondering if this guy at the other end of the line (Mike) was clairvoyant, and with no small amount of swallowed pride, the doctor put a lid on his inner sputtering and simply answered the question.

"Okay. Sit tight." Mike told him. "We'll be there as soon as we can." (Having driven down Rohdy Creek Truck Trail numerous times to pull out stranded motorists, Mike had strategically placed Coke and Pepsi cans on stumps in different sections of the road so he would know the best way to drive in with his truck.)

Mike then told us that "rowdy road" that day was so wet and muddy from the storm that had swept through the day before (the same storm that had chased the bikers into the Bear Trap Inn) that even he had had a hard time reaching this stranded couple, despite his truck's enormous tires. After Mike towed their car to the main road, the doctor commented how stupid he was to have driven down that road.

Mike told us he tried to reassure the guy by saying, "No, you're not stupid. You just made a mistake." But then, as if on cue, his wife chimed in to differ. "Yes," she insisted, "he *is* stupid! My husband is a very smart doctor but today, as a driver, stupid—very, very stupid." The guy sighed, paid Mike, and drove away in his mud-spattered car.

Having tucked away this treasure of a story, we figured we were done, but no, not quite. Mike proceeded to tell us about his first date with his wife, and how when they walked out of her house her eyes had widened in surprise when she saw he was driving his big tow truck, *with*, Mike added for emphasis, a car chained to the bed of it. In response, he told us, he grinned at her and said, "I figured you might as well get used to it."

About a week earlier, Mike added, his wife was mowing the lawn when the mower engine quit. So naturally, Mike told us with a proud smile, she took the motor apart to find out what was wrong and had asked him to pick her up a new starter. Just that very morning, Mike added, she had laid the broken starter on his end table near his glasses, and said, with a smile, "It sure would be nice to get that starter." (In that moment, I said to myself *I love this woman!)* Then, Mike finished his story by telling us he had picked up a used starter that very day and was planning to "surprise" her with it that night. What a fine new spin on romance!

Some final bits of treasure awaited us. As Mike was talking, I noticed his baptism certificate displayed proudly on the wall. Yet another unexpected endearing treasure was his business card in bright pink, homage to three different women in his and wife's families who had or have had breast cancer. That sealed the deal for me. I was ready to pack up and move north tomorrow just to be near this wonderful man and his fine-character friends who stood at the ready to help other people.

Thank you, Mike. Thank you, Sam, who plugged our temporary tire. Thank you, Sam's girlfriend. Thank you, biker pepper lover. Thanks, *da U.P.*, for the pocketful of treasures.

## *Questions to Ponder*

- As you think back to one of your favorite vacations, what are some of the great memories (treasures) you brought home?
- Can you think of a time when you had an out-of-the-ordinary experience that you judged instead of being open to it?
- Looking ahead to your next vacation, what kinds of true treasure would you most like to bring home?

V

# Good Habits Are Good Friends

Two sources of success are known: wisdom and effort; make them both thine own, if thou wouldst haply rise.

—Magha

CHAPTER 28

# Never Stop Asking Questions

ONE DAY AT church when I was five and a young first grader, I sat in a circle with other children my age for Sunday school, trying not to squirm. Our teacher, a mother who had either volunteered or whose arm had been twisted, was giving us a lesson. I don't recall the exact topic. A common approach back then, and probably one still in use today, was to tell a Bible-based fable and then try to jumpstart the kids into talking about it. What I do remember from that day was asking her questions. Even at so young an age, I had begun, in kid terms, to wonder about such large and puzzling concepts as God, the universe, and eternity. Although I have forgotten the exact details, I recall a back-and-forth volley such as the one below:

(Me) Q: How big is God?
(The teacher) A: As big as the universe.

Q: How big is the universe?
A: Very, very big.

Q: But what's outside the universe?
A: Nothing.

Q: How do we know?
A: Well, we don't. That's why God is God.

Q: But if God knows, why doesn't God tell us?
A: (After a pause and then with a thin, tight smile) Little girl, I think it's time you stopped asking questions.

The teacher's words seared in my brain: *It's time you stopped asking questions.* I knew, even at so young an age, there was something off about her words.

While drafting this chapter, I dug into a bit of history about the roots of Sunday school. Such schools, I learned, which were designed to help keep young boys out of trouble, led to the creation of state-run schools in England. Since then, the ways we educate young people have undergone enormous changes and will continue to evolve. One thing, though, has always been clear to me. The best teachers are those who ask probing questions and then, rather than spoon-feeding the answers, expect their students to think. The art of asking questions is also at the core of my passion for my work as a career and life coach. There is nothing so welcome as the pregnant pause I hear on the heels of a question I have asked, which, to me, is the sweet sound of someone possibly on the verge of a shift or even a breakthrough in awareness.

As I think about the power of questions, I zero in on a few of the important questions I have long held in the front of my mind:

- What are my true sources of happiness or wellbeing, and what are the best ways to tap into them?
- How can I be responsive to the needs of my family, friends, and the community, *and* be responsive to myself—my interests, my passions, and the things I yearn to do?
- How much do people change over time, and how do they do it?
- How, in a helpful, positive way, can I use the stark inevitability of death to further awaken and to savor life more fully?
- Living in a society whose economy depends on consumerism, how can I best be a steward of the earth's resources?
- Where is the healthy balance between being organized and work-focused and being spontaneous and having fun?

Most of the boys who attended fledgling Sunday schools worked in factories six days a week under deplorable conditions. By contrast, during my years of Sunday school, I lived in a loving home that my father built with his own hands in a neighborhood where neighbors knew everyone up and down the street and where kids could play safely outdoors with little or no supervision. I attended a good school with teachers I liked. In contrast to my Sunday schoolteacher that day, who certainly meant well, I was also blessed with a father who tended to ask rather than tell, who let his children make mistakes, and who guided rather than punished. Although my family didn't have much money when I was growing up (it was not easy for a man working on the floor of a machine shop to support a family of six), in contrast to the boys enrolled in those first Sunday schools, I see just how privileged I was and am.

One measure of that privilege is how I could see so clearly, on that Sunday morning so many years ago, how uncomfortable my teacher was with my questions. And even though I was only five years old, I knew with every fiber of my being that she was wrong–dead wrong. It is *never, ever* time to stop asking questions.

## *Questions to Ponder*

- What messages did you receive while you were growing up about asking questions? What messages would you like to give yourself now?
- What are two or three important questions you keep mulling over in your mind as the years pass?
- What's one situation in your life where you would benefit by asking more questions about it?
- In your connections with other people, what's one way you could be more compassionate and supportive by asking questions instead of giving advice?

CHAPTER 29

# Keep Putting Pen to Paper

ACCESSING A PHYSICAL mailbox today is quite a different experience than when letters were touched by many human hands before being retrieved by a family member or friend and then opened eagerly. Except for special occasions–birthdays, Mother's Day, Father's Day, and holidays in December (if those)–today's mailbox serves up a dreary menu of credit card solicitations, business mailings, requests for contributions from an unlimited number of worthy causes, and unwanted catalogs that breed like rabbits and thanks to pre-printing won't be the last one you'll receive (as I'm cheerily reminded whenever I call to ask to be removed from yet another mailing list). Most days I wonder *why bother?*

For this reason, I cherish the handwritten letters and cards I've received over the years, now lovingly tucked away in drawers and shoeboxes. I knew a woman who lost all her possessions in a house fire and eventually called it one of the best things that ever happened to her because it she had no choice but to make a fresh start. While admiring her courage and positive attitude, when I see photographs of people like her—women and men standing amidst the ruins of their homes, stooped over the charred rubble with a desperate hope of finding at least a few precious mementos—I shudder most over the thought of two losses that would feel unfathomable to me: family photos and my trove of cards and letters that I've sorted into several groupings.

## *Refrigerator postcards*

The first group worth mentioning are the vacation postcards that feature gorgeous landscapes. Some have been affixed to our refrigerator for well over ten years by a motley collection of magnets. They include photographs of a white stucco balcony in Greece overlooking the deep blue waters of the Mediterranean, an aerial photograph of lush mountains on the Nā Pali coast in Hawaii, an aerial photo of Coral Bay on St. John in the U.S. Virgin Islands, near the place where our older daughter and her husband were married and where, years ago, our combined families spent a week together, and a shot of the Cliffs of Moher in Ireland.

## *Special occasion cards*

Next up are the card collections, which I have sorted and placed into separate, sealable plastic bags: birthday cards (from my husband and daughters, and from friends on milestone birthdays, which I like to celebrate in grand fashion), anniversary cards, Valentine's Day cards, Mother's Day cards, cards given to me when I retired from the University of Michigan in 2011, and an assortment of others that mean so much to me I can't imagine getting rid of them. Both of my daughters, when they were younger, gave me handmade cards for my birthday and Mother's Day. Although I would never have expected this touching practice to last (at the same time as I also hold dear the many store-bought cards I have received), to this day the younger one designs and creates, by hand, many of the cards she gives to family members and close friends.

## *Letters from my then husband-to-be*

In the spring of 1975, a few months after I started seeing the man who would become my husband, he left for a six-week trip, planned months before we got together. On the day he left, how my heart ached! I wrote to him almost daily and sent batches of letters to the addresses of people he would be staying with along the way. In return, what I received each week was only a single postcard or short letter.

Young, vulnerable, and still unsure of this new love, I managed to convince myself that hearing from him only once a week was a sign that he didn't truly love me. (Only later would I understand that his writing to me *every single week*, more mail than he had ever sent to anyone in so short a time, meant quite the opposite.) That small packet of letters and postcards tied together with a ribbon means the world to me.

## *Letters from my daughters*

There's also a box of letters and postcards from our daughters over the more than ten years between when they first went to summer camp and when they enrolled in college.

This collection includes an amusing set of letters our older daughter sent during her first week at sleepover camp. Beginning on the second day of camp, some of her friends started receiving "care packages" from home. (I was completely in the dark about this practice.) Immediately our daughter sent a letter to us asking me to send her such a package. Subsequently, two or three more letters arrived, each one more strongly worded than the last, all of which I received *after* it was too late to send anything that would arrive before she left camp. The next year, as she prepared to return to camp, I began buying items well ahead of time to include in care packages for her. To compensate for the previous year, I sent two such packages. It was a small price to pay for once again receiving her usual cheerful missives home that I adored.

Years later, during her first year away at college, she sent me a letter that made me cry grateful tears. When our daughters were young, their grandmother, who worked part-time at a public library well into her seventies, regularly mailed used picture books to the girls, or brought them with her when she visited. Not surprisingly, these books were chock full of male characters and references. To counter this stereotype, I methodically, painstakingly blacked out the pronouns *he* and *him*, neatly replacing them with *she* and *her*. In a letter mailed to me that first year, my daughter wrote, "I get it now, Mom—why you spent all that time changing *he* to *she*, and I thank you so much!" (She eventually chose to major in Women's Studies.)

## *Letters from my father*

Among my handwritten treasures from earlier periods of my life are a precious few handwritten letters from my father. Even today, when I touch the tips of my fingers to his "Love, Dad" on the last page of each letter, I conjure a picture of him sitting at the dining room table, writing these closing words before folding the letter and tucking it into its envelope.

Sadly, I have not a single letter from my mother. After the movie *Billy Elliot* came out, I became a repeat watcher, which I don't often do. In a scene from the movie, Billy's ballet dance teacher (performed by the marvelous Julie Walters) reads aloud the letter Billy has brought to show her—the letter his mother wrote to him before she died. Every time I watch this scene, I begin to cry, tears born from a deep hunger for such a letter from my own mother. But I have also come to understand how much strength it would have taken for Mom to have written such letters to her children. To have done such a thing, especially during the last year of her life as her cancer progressed, would have required her to nudge open the door to death and the unfathomable reality of leaving behind her precious children. With this understanding, I have found solace in the writing of hers I do have, which includes only some recipe cards and an old address book with the neat, straight lines she drew through the names of people who moved away or died. Meager as these written words are, I am deeply grateful to have them.

## *Letters from my "Brudda"*

(When one of our cousins was a young girl her family nicknamed her Sister, pronounced in a Vermont accent as Sistah. For many years, my brother Peter has called me Sistah, conjuring up for himself a male counterpart: Brudda.)

During 1967–68, when I was in my last year of high school and Peter was in his first year at the University of Vermont, he wrote quite faithfully to me (especially for an eighteen-year-old guy): three- and four-page letters written in his distinctive block print. As I think back on how much those letters meant to me, gratitude washes over me. Although he and I have never talked about it, I expect he knew how hard it was for me to be left behind for one final year of enduring my stepmother's ways before making my long-yearned-for escape into the rest of my life. Those letters–a lifeline to the bond with my brother–helped tether me to my true self, and no matter how many times I downsize, I could never let them go.

## *Letters from my friend Susan*

Letters from Susan, penned in her elegant handwriting with its big, bold loops, are among my handwritten treasures. Any college friendship that's remained intact for more than forty years is, by its nature, priceless, one whose value has been maintained by phone calls and a collection of letters over the years. As time passed and our lives with children and families grew ever busier, the distance between our letters to each other also widened. But even after many months or even a few years of no contact, a letter from Susan would make its way faithfully to my mailbox, whether in Oregon, Iowa, or, eventually, Michigan.

Each letter brought news about the latest installment of Susan's life: her mother's early and tragic death, getting married, giving birth to her eldest daughter, divorce, buying a home, adopting her younger daughter. Her letters also mentioned books she told me I simply *must* read as well as news about mutual friends. These letters, which mark Susan as a true and lasting friend, are good as gold.

## *Finding my parents' love letters*

About ten years ago while my husband and I were visiting my brother Peter and sister-in-law Martha in Vermont, my brother mentioned a box of family letters in their attic, hinting somewhat guiltily that they had been in storage there for many years and that he had forgotten to mention them to me. In response, I practically leapt out of my chair, dragging him upstairs to find the box.

Among handwritten prized possessions, this was the Mother Lode (and, in this case, Father): hundreds of letters our parents had mailed to each other during the two times they were apart. The first was the year Mom attended normal school (at that time a three-year teacher preparatory training for young women) when she and Dad wrote to each other at least twice a week. The second was when, as a member of the Civil Conservation Corps, our father-to-be had no choice but to work away from home.

Because my mother died before I had a chance to get to know her as a person, being able to glimpse these times of her life was a gift beyond measure. Some of the letters show my mother at her best. They reveal her as being fully engaged in many aspects of life that as kids we didn't see. While she was in high school, she played on the basketball team, taught Sunday school, was an excellent student (valedictorian of her small class), and had many close friends. As our mother, she struggled to keep up with even the most basic activities of a homemaker and seemed unable to do many of the things other mothers in the neighborhood did, such as plant flowers in the yard. Other letters expose a deep-seated insecurity that saddened me. Family legend has it that on the one and only day my father forgot to kiss Mom goodbye when he left for work, she was in tears for most of the day, afraid Dad was upset with her.

I will always wonder what muffled my mother's vibrant, self-assured side that was so alive in her youth. Might it have been postpartum depression never diagnosed or treated? The challenges of staying home with children? This question will never find an answer, but the picture, through these love letters, of a time in my mother's life when she was fully engaged has found a welcome and permanent home in my mind.

## *Special thanks to three great role models*

I must mention three favorite role models for sending cards and letters. The first is my Grammie Haskell, who sent birthday cards to each of her twenty-two grandchildren up until the year each of them turned twelve. To each birthday card she taped a quarter. (In my thirties, I sent a birthday card to one of my brothers with two taped quarters. Next to the second one, I wrote "Inflation.")

My second is Dr. David Bloom, chair of the department of urology at the University of Michigan. Among his many fine traits, Dr. Bloom is well known and appreciated for sending handwritten notes. He also happens to have beautiful handwriting and writes his notes with fine ink pens on simple, elegant stationery. During my years at the University, I received several notes from David, all a permanent part of my collection. When I hold them in my hand, I feel his compassion, his attention, his caring, and his uplifting energy. How could I ever throw them away?

My other favorite role model is my younger daughter, Janelle, who, at the time of this writing, lived in New York City, where her father was born and grew up, which leads me to a story that inspired this chapter. (I must add here that in no way do these comments imply any favoritism between her and her older sister, both of whom I love completely and without condition.)

Shortly after Labor Day in the fall of 2007, the girls' grandmother, a lifelong, fiercely proud, and loyal New Yorker, fell and broke her hip while walking down a few short steps after leaving a family celebration at a restaurant. After a string of doctor visits that went from bad to worse, and with a heart made heavy by leaving behind her beloved NYC, she agreed to let us move her to Michigan, where my husband and I, with our daughters grown and more or less on their own, were able to give her the support she needed, as well as access to excellent health care.

With my mother-in-law now living more than six hundred miles from the city, Janelle decided to send her a series of postcards with photos of the city, historical as well as modern. Initially, she planned to send one each month, but given the busy life she was leading (and still leads), this goal proved to be overly ambitious. Nevertheless, over the next five-and-a-half years, ending with the final postcard that arrived just a few days after her grandmother's death, our daughter sent twenty-five postcards (along with a few cards and one typed letter).

Words can't describe the pleasure her grandmother took from every one of those postcards. After a postcard arrived, it would sit on the end table next to her wine-colored La-Z-Boy chair for a few weeks, or even longer. Some found their way to the bulletin board next to her desk or taped to the wall near her chair. As it was my job once a week or so to bring some order to the ever-growing, chaotic piles of my mother-in-law's catalogs, library books, and other mail stacked here and there in her apartment, I made sure Janelle's postcards found their way to a stack of personal cards and correspondence that I named The Happy Pile.

Every time my mother-in-law received another postcard, she said, "That girl can get more on a single postcard than most people can fit into a whole letter." It was true; Janelle wrote in print so small she could share lots of news.

Almost seven years after we moved my mother-in-law to Michigan, she died at the age of ninety-four. A year later, during the weeks leading up to the December holidays, I painstakingly compiled a bulging book called *Postcards to Grandma*. On the left side of each fold was pasted the front of the actual postcard and on the opposite page was a photocopy of the back of the post-card, printed on heavy paper stock to make it feel and look like the original postcard. More than just a book of postcards, this binder was testimony to the power of love–treasure indeed. [How sweet!]

Since I place such high value on my own collection of cards and letters, I do my best to contribute to other's (whether or not they save them). I send birthday cards (some of my family would add *not always on time* and they would be right), sympathy cards, and thank you notes. Do I have a perfect track record? Far from it.

Still and ever, I feel satisfied and happy when I slide letters and cards into the slot of a post office box or place them in our mailbox and then raise the red metal flag to alert the delivery person of outgoing mail. Feel free to call me old fashioned. In the years to come, as more and more ways to communicate electronically, and with ever-greater speed, are born, I suggest nevertheless that in even small ways we continue occasionally, to put pen to paper, to write out the person's address by hand (no printed labels for me), to affix a stamp, and then send the card or letter on its deliciously slow way. I have paused here to celebrate my boxes in the attic of written treasures. I end by wishing for each of you such a trove of your own.

## *Questions to Ponder*

- What's one way you could occasionally send a handwritten card or letter to someone special in your life?
- Are there any collections of letters in your family you might enjoy looking through?
- In this age, when electronic communication is so pervasive, what's one thing you could do to personalize and add a human touch to some of your communications with family and close friends (e.g., through services that allow you to create personalized cards, photo albums, or even books)?
- Is there a way for you to print and store some of the more special electronic communications you receive (notes that, in spirit, are the kind of letters people received in their mailboxes before the electronic age) so that you treat them as the treasure they are?

CHAPTER 30

# Stop Swearing, Dabnabit

*Some of the lessons in this book came to me a long time ago and, like loyal friends, have stayed with me. But a few lessons, such as this one, bubbled up during the writing process as if by invitation.*

My parents, who were religious, church-going people, did not use profanity. Neither did my brothers. So, swearing was not something I grew up around. A case in point is from a day when I was in my early twenties. I announced to my father I wanted to be cremated when I died. He looked at me for a moment, sighed, and said, "Glenda, if you die before I do, for the first time in my life I'm going to do with you what I damn well please."

I remember this brief exchange for a few reasons—for the way it made me laugh out loud, for my father's straight face, and for just how hard it is at times to be a parent. But another reason I remember that scene so vividly is because my father had used a swear word, albeit a mild one. I kid you not, this is the only time my father swore in my presence (and believe me there were more than a few situations when I gave him good reasons to swear).

But despite growing up in a curse-free home, somehow over the years I fell into the habit of swearing. Don't get me wrong; it wasn't as if our daughters heard me swear a lot. Typically, I was alone in the car or out of earshot. Even then, I did my best to swear quietly, under my breath.

I have one especially embarrassing story. One day I was driving to the grocery store with our younger daughter securely strapped into her car seat behind me. She was three years old. As we approached a traffic light at a busy intersection, I became annoyed, probably by a slow-to-respond driver–one of my pet peeves–and I said (under my breath, I thought), "Sh*t." Turns out it wasn't far enough under my breath to escape my daughter's finely tuned ears. (Perhaps even then she was showing early signs of musical talent.) From the backseat came her innocent, small voice repeating over and over, rhythmically, as if she were rolling it around in her mouth like a piece of hard candy: "Sh*it, sh*it, sh*it, sh*t."

In the front seat, shame colored my cheeks a deep rose. After all, since *I* had just used the word, what sense did it make to tell my daughter in that moment that she wasn't allowed to use it? So, I decided to leave well enough alone, swearing to myself (sic) to never do it again and to have a conversation with her when the time was right.

For a woman with a lifelong passion for language and words, cursing makes no sense. It's inarticulate, crude, and mindless. For a few years in my late teens and early twenties, I smoked cigarettes. I will never forget the time a friend said to me, after watching me light up, "I didn't know you smoked. You seem far too intelligent for that." Ouch. (Shortly after meeting my future husband, I quit smoking. He wouldn't have stayed with me if I hadn't, and my choice was a no-brainer.) The same kind of connection between intelligence and swearing can be made easily. If I'm as smart as I like to think I am, why do I swear?

During the first few years after I retired from my career, I spent a good deal of time at home, often alone, as my husband continued to work full-time. One day I realized I had unconsciously begun to talk to myself during the day when I was alone in the house. (Such talking out loud is likely more common than people dare to admit.) After all, company is nice and I was the only one around. Because talking to oneself is generally viewed as a sign that something isn't right, at least before ear buds and Bluetooth technology became so prevalent, I felt a little crazy when I realized what I was doing.

At the same time, I discovered I was cursing more often, and that this unworthy habit seemed to be spreading like a virus into other areas of my life, too. (Again, I'm exaggerating. There's a continuum of swear words I will never see the far end of.) Having grown up in a curse-free family, I was unhappy to find I had become a person who swears.

*Why,* I asked myself, *was I swearing so much*? What was it about? Having grown up as the only girl and youngest in my family, perhaps I came to see swearing as a way to stand up for myself. Much later, in my early twenties and as a child of the sixties, I proudly identified myself as a hippie and a feminist (the latter identity has only strengthened over time). Perhaps I took to sprinkling the F-word into my speech here and there as proof that I was willing to break the rules. Okay. I get all that. But fast-forward forty years, and there I was, happily walking around our lovely home swearing far too often. What was up with that? After thinking it over, I decided to apply a powerful tool I have used in other important areas of my life—to go cold turkey, to completely give up swearing.

At first, it was tough. Curse words just tumbled out of my mouth in the same way all habits (bad and good) conscript the brain. But soon I began to catch myself. Between the thought and the words coming out of my mouth, a middle step showed up that let me put the brakes on. When a swear word slipped out, I quickly spoke tamer words out loud. Darn it. Goodness. Drat. Brothuh. (The last one was my paternal grandfather's favorite expression of disgust, spoken in his distinct blend of a Maine-Vermont accent.)

As the weeks passed, I found myself forming—yes, a new habit. New words. Milder words. Gentler words. Plus, I found that my tendency to swear began to naturally drop away. I even came up with an endearing term for inanimate, guiltless objects that had "done something" I found to be annoying, such as a fork falling on the floor. They became *buddy.* If an object fell out of my hands, I said to it as if it were a friend *come on buddy,* and then picked it up.

I was pleasantly surprised to experience a side benefit: the less I swore, the less angry I felt and the more matter-of-factly I started responding to frustrations and inconveniences. One morning when I knocked over my water bottle onto the rug, I said nothing and calmly walked downstairs to get a towel. It turned out swearing wasn't the release from anger and frustration I had always thought it to be. At times, it may have been the cause of it. Having largely freed myself from swearing, I also let go of a lot of anger–a valuable lesson indeed.

*Postscript.* I recently learned about the work of Dr. Timothy Jay, professor of psychology at the Massachusetts College of Liberal Arts, who many consider to be an expert on swearing. Based on his research, Jay has said that within some contexts swearing has been shown to be beneficial. Still, I'll stick with my commitment because I think it's the best way for me to give up a bad habit. When it comes to swearing, I have found it hard, I confess, not to fall back into groove-worn habits. But every effort to change a bad habit looks the same: climb on the wagon, fall off, and repeat as often as necessary. Dabnabit, don't we wish it were easier?

## *Questions to Ponder*

- Is there a time during the past month or so when you used profanity or negative words in a way you later regretted? What might you learn from your experience?
- When you listen to other people swearing, how does it make you feel? What impression of the person does it leave you with?
- If you want to swear less, what strategies might work best for you?

CHAPTER 31

# Wear Good Raingear—Inside and Out

AFTER I RETIRED and while my husband was still working, twice a week he and I would go on a forty-minute walk early in the morning. On those days, my husband climbed out of bed at five a.m. while I slept an extra twenty-five minutes. Right on schedule, a few minutes after six a.m., we went outside and locked the door behind us. The morning I wrote this chapter, it was raining and I don't mean just a sprinkle. The rain was coming down in a steady pour. On such a day, most people of sane mind would climb back into bed, but not us.

As people who love the outdoors, we own clothing for almost any type of weather, including a wide range of layers to stay warm in winter, wide-brimmed hats for kayaking, hiking boots, mosquito net hats that drape down over our faces and shoulders (which is so annoying to wear I put it on only when I feel utterly miserable), and, of course, good raingear. So, that morning we donned raincoats, rain pants, and rain hats, topped off with reflector bibs, and headed out into the rain.

There was nothing particularly eventful about our walk. We passed by the same houses with their lights on and many more houses and apartments still enveloped in darkness. With visibility poor on such a wet morning, even though as walkers we had the right of way, we hung back at a four-way stop to let drivers pass before crossing the glistening street that reflected the overhead streetlights.

We somewhat reluctantly made another concession to the weather. On Traver Boulevard near the entrance to Leslie Golf Course, where the road turned to dirt, we decided to turn around. At that time of year, the road that passes through the two sides of the golf course is ridged and pockmarked with potholes, which, when it rains, becomes an obstacle course. Even if we had successfully dodged the winding stretch of puddles that resembled a moonscape with the diffuse backdrop light from the city reflecting off the muddy water, our feet would almost certainly soon be drenched, despite good wool socks inside supposedly waterproof hiking boots. We were hardy but not dumb. Back at the house, dripping, we trudged down the basement stairs, peeled off our wet layers, and hung up each dripping piece. Heading back upstairs, we agreed there was something particularly satisfying about a walk in the pouring rain.

*What is it,* I wondered, *that made it such a feel-good thing*? The sheer enjoyment of being outdoors, come what may? Feeling like kids again? The reassuring rhythm of raindrops as they were dripping from the brims of our hats onto our raincoats? The keen sense of solitude, knowing that even the occasional runner we usually pass on these walks isn't out on such a morning? Or is it the reflection of strength of character in not being stopped by the rain?

As I pondered this walk, plumbing it for lessons, it came to me that throughout life we all encounter situations where we challenge ourselves or when others ask us to go out into "bad weather." In addition to outer raingear, over time we also acquire inner raingear. For me, one of the joys of coaching is helping people–in their good weather and bad–to figure out a strategy and take steps to follow it. My clients dig through their inner "wardrobes," don the appropriate gear, and head out the door. And when they come back for the next session, we pause for high fives, and then turn our heads to look up the road for what's next on the horizon, rain or shine.

When is appropriate inner raingear essential?

- When we face a task or chore we're not interested in doing or even dread, good raingear helps us dig in anyway, as we accept delayed gratification.
- When kids try our patience by having "bad weather" days, good raingear reminds us of how impressionable children are and how essential it is for us to show them the way.

- When we take a risk, such as interviewing for a new job or taking the initiative to reach out to someone we don't know well, good raingear gives us courage.
- When we stick to a discipline, such as a writing practice or regular exercise, even when we're in a slump, good raingear helps convince us to stay the course and believe in ourselves.
- When we speak up for what we believe is right, especially in the face of people who disagree, good raingear gives us strength and confirms our most important values.

But there was a second important lesson from that morning walk in the rain. Just as my husband and I did that morning, where we have a choice, it's not only okay it's *smart* to avoid walking down dirt roads full of potholes--especially in the pouring rain. So, my friends, as Gene Kelley sang so famously, here's to (sometimes) "dancin' and singin' in the rain."

## *Questions to Ponder*

- What "inner rain gear" do you already have in your "closet?"
- What additional inner rain gear would you would like to hang there?
- What might you do to make that happen?

CHAPTER 32

# Lesson from a Friend—from Slush to Sure

One morning I was having tea and enjoying easy conversation with a friend when, at a pause in our conversation, I commented that we weren't "getting much done." Flashing one of her broad, beautiful smiles, she said, "That's okay because this is *slush time."* I had a cascade of thoughts after her comment about my long-standing struggle between my intense outer drive to be productive and my inner yearning for more downtime.

I have long tortured myself with a persistent, loud-mouthed *should* to take charge of my own calendar, as if calling in the military to turn anarchy into order. I have tried and failed, tried and failed again. Many years ago, I enrolled in a Franklin Planner class, excited by the promise of a new, more efficient me. My office ordered a year's supply of pages for my new planner and even sprang for the costlier set with a background motif of spring flowers in muted pastel colors. Finally, I thought, I had found a planning system that would work for me.

The beginning of day one after my class, my Franklin Planner transformation went well. Following the step-by-step prescription that I'd received in class, I created a long to-do list along, with multiple sub-actions, and dutifully assigned a priority number to each one. But despite my wellspring of hope and good intention, by six p.m., when it was time for me to turn out the light and head home, although I had gotten a great deal of work done, as I reviewed the detailed list in my planner I placed completion checkmarks by only two of the items. The rest of the long list stared back at me disdainfully, as if calling me such names as *disorganized, hopeless, loser.*

By day three, when a single to-do item consumed almost the entire day, I was tempted to hold a lit match, or better yet a torch, to the corner of those empty, accusing, flower-laden pages, freeing myself from this time-management prison I had idiotically checked myself into. I imagined myself inside a room like the ones I remembered from television shows I watched when I was a kid. Someone, typically the person who would later turn out to be the hero, was trapped inside a very small room whose walls suddenly began to move in slowly, giving him or her only minutes to escape being crushed. The planner system felt like walls closing in on me, but instead of letting myself be crushed, within a couple of weeks I hid both the planner and all those lovely pages in the back of my desk drawer. One evening a year or two later, after everyone else had left for the day, like an accused person destroying evidence I buried all those blank planner pages at the bottom of the recycle bin.

So, it went. As a person who has always gotten a lot done and who prides myself on doing good work, I received several good promotions during my years at the university. In my own way, I was doing a lot right. Thinking back on it, I credit my success to a mix of three things: a strong work ethic passed down from my father, stoic New England blood coursing through my veins (for which there is not a shred of scientific evidence) and an underlying fear of failure mixed with a dash of imposter theory (*one of these days they will find out the truth about me*). Despite my accomplishments, I continued to berate myself for a failure to have (and *use*) a good system for allocating hours in the day.

Over the years I've read more than a few books about time management. For a week or so I was a convert of David Allen's excellent *Getting Things Done* system. Despite my own failure to put his system into practice, to this day I recommend his book to people. I also studied the insightful book *It's About Time: The Six Styles of Procrastination and How to Overcome Them* by Linda Sapadin and Jack Mcguire, which is by far my favorite book on that painful subject. My favorite book, which I have continued to pull down from the shelf and reread every few years, is *Time Management for Unmanageable People: The Guilt-Free Way to Organize, Energize, and Maximize Your Life* by Ann McGee-Cooper. The first time I read Ann's book, I kept thinking to myself *finally someone understands me!* Through her book, she gave me permission to be myself in how I organize my time, something we all crave.

When I retired in 2011, one of the things I looked forward to most was open time in my days and freedom over how to spend it. To use my friend's term, I relished the idea of having more slush time. But when people asked, "How's retirement?" all I could do was laugh because other than the switch to being my own boss, not much had changed. As much as ever, I drove myself relentlessly toward getting more done in a day than seemed humanly possible.

Why, I wondered a few weeks later, had I been so ferociously averse to any kind of system for allocating my time? One possible answer is that I cannot stand being boxed in. As a decidedly "unmanageable" ENFP type on the Myers-Briggs Type Inventory (Extrovert-Intuitive-Feeling-Perceiving), I can talk to people forever, friends and strangers alike; I'm a forest kind of gal (vs. trees); I wear my heart on my sleeve–emotional highs being, as I see it, worth the price of emotional lows that come along for the ride; and the image of someone else's empty desk with papers filed away into neatly labeled folders sends me into a panic. As one of my clients playfully named it, I'm a *piler*, not a *filer*.

While being coached several years ago, the light bulb inside my brain began to shine light on this problem. Instead of constraining me, of boxing me in, maybe, just maybe, assigning specific times in my day to specific activities might be *liberating*. How so? Because then I could stop spending so much mental energy on it. I could stop "shoulding" on myself, stop feeling guilty, stop being weighed down by *not doing*. As Rex Harrison's 'enry 'ggins in the 1964 movie *My Fair Lady* so famously said, "By George, she's got it!"

One morning while editing in the Beanery Café at the Michigan League on the campus of the University of Michigan, I looked out through the bank of tall windows facing North University Avenue. Why was I there? Because for more than a year I had made and kept writing dates with myself: two two-hour blocks every Tuesday and Thursday morning. Because that day was a Thursday and because I had designated the eight a.m. to ten a.m. timeslot on my calendar to writing, there we sat, dutifully, my computer and I. Over a long series of those appointments with myself (which I eventually doubled to four-hour blocks) over four years I drafted more than sixty chapters, which I'm in the process of editing the heck out (with great professional help) in the final stages leading up to the publication of this book.

Don't get me wrong. I still love healthy slush time. Always will. That's a good thing. I'll never be the kind of person whose schedule is booked solid from morning till night, not this ENFP woman. But even though I'll never be a Franklin Planner or David Allen disciple, I have come up with a system for moving from unhelpful *slush* (doing nothing) to *sure* (making it happen), one that involves three simple steps. Every Monday morning, I write down on an index card my intentions (goals) for the week. Then, on pages in a small, spiral-bound notebook, at the top of each page for the coming seven days I write the day of the week and date, to which I then add lists of daily intentions—the things I plan to accomplish each day. Finally, for certain types of activities (such as my twice weekly writing dates), I designate times on my electronic calendar. In my mind, these are appointments with my intentions.

Thanks to this simple but effective system, I *will* bring this book into print, hopefully before the year is out (I won't say which year I had in mind when I first wrote those words). Plus, on other fronts I *will* play my sweet little lady of a ukulele named May-Belle, meditate, take walks, and see friends—all through a planning and action process that liberates me, one that ties me tangibly to what's most important. However, as an ENFP type, there will always be times when I veer away from my list of intentions into other activities not on any of my lists. It's who am I. When this happens, I use a little trick. I add these activities to my list as if I had meant to include all along, and then, with a flourish of the pen, I mark them as done with a satisfying strikethrough.

Do I have any advice for you about how to move from (unhelpful) slush to sure? Nope. But I do know if this ENFP woman can figure out a system for making this happen, so can you.

## *Questions to Ponder*

- Is there a system for getting things done (or something else in life) you've been trying to force yourself into using?
- What's at least one good reason it's not working for you?
- If you were to custom design a time-management process for yourself, what would it look like?

CHAPTER 33

# Lessons from Karl

ONE MORNING I sat on a sturdy oak chair at the Ann Arbor public library, at an equally sturdy table designed to give four people ample space to spread out books and papers. That day it felt especially lonely at the table because our dear friend Karl had died.

As the owner of the Shaman Drum Bookshop, one of the best independent stores in the country for more than twenty-five years, Karl read books—a *lot* of books. For many years, at the beginning of every semester long lines of students snaked out the door, down the stairs, and along the sidewalk. The profit from textbook sales was the bookstore's bread and butter, allowing it to hold fast to its scholarly mission. Over time, though, as the Internet pushed its way into every corner of our lives, the hours students spent in line at Karl's bookstore and others in town may have been part of what pushed them to urge the university to require faculty to provide textbook lists in advance, online. In the first September after this change happened, the lines at Shaman Drum slowed to a trickle. Almost overnight the days of long lines at Ann Arbor bookstores at the beginning of each semester were gone—and, with them, a lifeblood stream of revenue for the Drum.

Although this change was bound to happen, I can imagine how hard it must have been for the many faculty who valued the intellectual breadth and depth of the Drum, and who regularly purchased books there and attended the bookshop's public readings that featured notable authors and poets, as well as distinguished but less well-known university faculty. To have pressed send while transmitting their public textbook lists for the first time must have felt like throwing darts not only at this literary bookstore they were so loyal to, but at Karl himself, who, to many of them, was also a good friend.

In the bookstore's final days, a continuous parade of friends and strangers descended on the bookshop like well-meaning locusts (each day offered an additional ten percent off), leaving with heavy bags full of books. Nonetheless, Karl and his wife Dianne ended up hauling many boxes of books home with them. Today, a few years after Karl died, thousands of books still sit like silent witnesses on the bookshelves in the home he shared with Dianne—finely constructed, hardwood shelves that once graced the bookstore. Even though Karl, with his own rich library at home, used public libraries less than most people, I know he would have liked it there at the library that day, surrounded by row after row of tall bookshelves–the stacks, as we fondly refer to them. My heart ached from wishing he were there.

A few months earlier, it had been my privilege to attend a sitting-and-walking meditation organized by and for Karl. It took place at the home of his friend, whose house sits simply, elegantly on a hill overlooking a bend in the Huron River. The house's wide sweeping windows drew in so much of the outdoors it took my breath away. After meditation, we gathered around a large island in the middle of the kitchen, drinking coffee, tea, or orange juice and eating the food Karl brought with him—bagels with cream cheese, pastries. Leave it to ever-thoughtful Karl to have brought the food.

As a parting gift, Karl handed each of us a photocopy of the Buddhist verse "Evening Gatha."

Let me respectfully remind you,
life and death
are of extreme importance.
Time swiftly passes by
and opportunity is lost.
Each of us should strive to awaken.
Awaken. Take heed.
Do not squander your life.

When someone we love dies, we reflect on the time we shared. Wanting to capture the details that typically escape us, we zoom in for a more careful look. We slow down the memories, savor them, and try to store pictures and sounds firmly away in the reaches of our minds, knowing how quickly memories fade and never, ever wanting to let them go. In the Jewish faith, there's a belief that our souls live on in the memories of others. That day, while writing at the library, I made an oath to carry my friend Karl with me for the rest of my life.

After the meditation, I affixed the "Evening Gatha" to the side of our refrigerator at eyelevel. It was a prayer I wanted to spend time with, to plant in my heart and mind. At that time, also affixed to our refrigerator was a photograph of Karl and Dianne with their two daughters and their families. With Karl's whole family in mind, I created a list of the top five lessons I learned from Karl.

*1. Read, read, read.*

A magnet on our refrigerator offers up these words of advice, printed in the foreground of a comic drawing: "Bad TV–Read a Book." A couple of years ago, when I was thinning out kid stuff that has been stored too long, I sent a message to our daughters to ask if either of them wanted a Mary Engelbreit poster, "Books Fall Open—You Fall In." Our younger daughter's reply leapt onto the screen, "I want it!"

Surely reading is one of the great pleasures of being human. I do not begrudge young people their videogames. But as I look back fondly on my weekly visits as a kid to the public library for another stack of books and the fun I had creating cocoon-like reading spaces, I can't help but believe that something big is lost when so many people spend so much time playing video games and so little time reading books.

Asking, "What are you reading these days?" was Karl's way of saying hello. I miss hearing him ask me the question, miss giving him my answer, and miss hearing about the book or books he was currently "falling into." Karl's breadth of reading often pushed me outside my comfort zone in my choice of books. Although books educate and entertain us, they also play a crucial role in how they help us strive to awaken.

*2. Support independent bookstores.*

I wish I had shopped more often at Shaman Drum. Too often, I fell prey to the sales tables in front of Border's Bookshop (long since gone out of business after it became a chain and eventually lost its way) and wandered inside, rarely coming out empty-handed. There is a place for both chain bookstores and independents, which might not be strong on the bargains, but I believe now more than ever they are jewels in our community we need to safeguard.

Independent bookstores give us the hands-on experience of being among physical books—the sweet feel of a book spine in the hand and the way a book's pages open for the first time. Like the Drum, many independent bookstores offer readings and other community events. One of my favorite sections of independent bookstores, which can often be found, is called Staff Picks, which encourage me to sample "dishes" from the grand smorgasbord of books being published. For me, there is also something mystical about walking into one—the sigh that escapes from me when I enter, the way my breath slows, the sense of quiet that sometimes feels, to me, like being in a sacred setting.

When my husband and I still dreamed of owning a second house in Vermont, for two main reasons we set our sights on Montpelier, Vermont's capital. First, we have much-loved family living there, but just as importantly this town of fewer than eight thousand people boasts *five* independent bookstores, showing without a doubt it's our kind of town.

Now, whenever we travel, I try to honor Karl's memory by visiting independent bookstores. During the first year after his death I bought books at Christopher's Books on 18$^{th}$ Street in Potrero Hill, San Francisco, the Flying Pig Bookstore in Shelburne, Vermont, and a sprinkling of bookstores in Ann Arbor, including Literati Bookstore, a smart little independent bookshop on the corner of Fourth Street and Washington, just one of numerous such gems in Ann Arbor.

Let us unite, those of us who are able, to help keep independent bookstores alive and in our midst. They are an important part of the lifeblood of our communities. Reflecting on the "Evening Gatha," independent bookstores may be an opportunity that, without our support, could be lost.

*3. Keep returning to the mat.*

Karl was a long-time student of Buddha and Zen and, like many, an off-again, on-again meditator. During a conversation with Karl one day, he touched on how essential it is to "keep returning to the mat," a rich metaphor we can apply not only to meditation but to all kinds of activities we stop doing but eventually begin again. As Karl talked about this practice, his voice resonated with deep compassion. Another metaphor I've heard meditation teachers use is to treat training the mind as if training a puppy. When the mind strays, like you would with a puppy bring it back to the mat. No anger. No scolding. Simply pick up the puppy and return it to the paper. Over and over, simply keep returning to the mat.

*4. Take naps.*

Karl loved naps. Often when we would see Karl at dinner group every other Sunday, he had the look of a rested man, his eyelids soft and slightly puffy, his mouth relaxed, his eyes clear and filled with ease. Although not much of a napper myself, which I admit is starting to change as I get older, I've always loved the idea of naps. A professor at the University of Michigan I once worked with on a project told people unabashedly about the twenty-minute nap he had in his office every afternoon. When I think of Karl, I think of a man who knew the wisdom of taking naps. Be good to yourselves, I hear him tell us. Although it may seem counterintuitive, naps help us to take heed, to awaken.

*5. Do not squander your life.*

The fifth and final lesson comes straight from the "Evening Gatha" like a loving arrow. To squander is to spend, to fritter away, to consume. When each day is gone, it's gone. While writing this chapter, it came to me that every breath I take has a number and my final breath, too, will have an unknown final number. Regardless of how young or old we are, we can never know where the current breath falls in relation to that final count. How many breaths do I have remaining? I cannot know. For this reason, more than savoring each day, it's important to savor each breath. In, out, in, out. *Use your days well,* I hear Karl whisper to me.

I will, my friend. I promise you. I will.

## *Questions to Ponder*

- What does how you currently spend your time say about you?
- What are the ways you may be squandering your life?
- At the end of your life, what do you want to be able to say about how you spent your time? About what you learned?
- What's one change you could commit to that will make it more likely you'll be content with how you used your time?

CHAPTER 34

# Lessons from Mom

Two days after Thanksgiving in 2012, "Mom," my beloved mother-in-law, left this world. At ninety-four, she had lived a good, long life and was, as she put it, "ready to go." As deaths go, hers was a good one. Right up to the end she was well cared for by the loving staff at Glacier Hills, a senior living community in Ann Arbor, experienced almost no pain, and passed away surrounded by family, her older son (my husband) on one side and a granddaughter (my older daughter) on the other, holding her hands.

Since one important way to keep the spirit of loved ones alive is through our memories, I want to share with you four of the most valuable lessons I learned from Mom during the thirty-seven years she was in my life. A couple of these lessons are from stories she loved to tell over and over, whereas others are based on things she said to me only once, but all of them are lessons I will continue to carry with me and do my best to live by.

*1. Two powerful words of advice*

Mom liked to say that someone once gave her some good advice about how to get along well with your kids after they grow up and have lives of their own. She shared this wisdom with me so many times I lost count. It's two short, simple words that offer excellent wisdom for all of us in lots of different situations: Shut up.

When I'm riding in the car with my husband and am tempted to suggest a different route (who's behind the wheel, after all?), when I see my kids doing anything that I would do differently (they're not the least bit interested), when my strong political views rush headlong from my brain toward my mouth when I know the only effect they would have is to further polarize (get off the soapbox before it's too late). These are but a few examples of the hundreds of times I have followed Mom's sage advice.

*2. Weddings or funerals—you choose*

This is a rule for life Mom mentioned to me only once many years ago, but my husband and I have lived by it ever since. "Whenever you're invited to family weddings," she said, "go!" Why? "Because," she continued, "weddings are happy occasions, and if you don't go to them [and other joyful family events] the only time you'll see your family is at funerals." (Early on my husband and I added Bar and Bat Mitzvahs to our list of happy occasions.) Over the years, we've invested a considerable amount in making sure the whole family has been an active part of happy occasions. This decision has proved to be, as the credit card advertisement says, priceless.

*3. Me? Old?*

Mom loved to say, "Old is ten years older than you are." What a fabulous attitude about aging. (I confess, though, that when she turned ninety, despite her still-young-at-heart attitude, I saw her as having officially crossed the threshold into old age. But naturally I never told *her* that. After all, by her formula the new old had simply rolled ahead another decade to the century mark itself.)

There's a related story Mom liked to tell. One day, while walking down the street (I believe she was in her seventies at the time—by her standards still a young woman), she saw a reflection in a store window. "Who in the world," she wondered, "is that old lady?" Then, in a flash, it came to her: *she* was the old lady in the window. At that point in the story, she liked to add, with a smile, "But then I realized that inside I still felt just as young as ever."

*4. How to let yourself get caught.*

This last lesson came from one of my final conversations with Mom less than a week before she died. While visiting her by myself, I asked her to tell me about the highlights of her life. Despite being extremely weak, a sweet smile lit up her face as she replied, "Meeting Jack [her husband]." When I asked her which of them had first felt the tug of romance, she smiled again and said softly, "As they say, I chased him until he caught me."

When something is important to us, we need to chase it—and be willing to invest whatever it takes to make it happen. But, as Mom reminded me in this final lesson, sometimes the best thing for us to do is to relax and let ourselves "get caught."

Thanks, Mom. I miss you and love you.

## *Questions to Ponder*

- What's one situation in your life where it would behoove you and others around you if you were to hold your tongue more often?
- What one thing you do to make yourself younger in spirit?
- Is there a "rule in life" you would like to commit to observing in your life?
- If a close friend or family member were to write a chapter like this about you, which lessons would they be likely to include?

CHAPTER 35

# Tap the Power of Black-and-White Decisions

For most of my life I've been a junkie for sweets. I was the person who, when a sheet cake showed up in the conference room at work to celebrate an event, salivated for the corner piece with extra frosting along both edges *and* the decorative rose on top. I loved sweets of every shape and kind: brownies, cookies, ice cream, M&Ms (peanut and plain), almost every candy bar ever made, and, best of all, dark chocolate, eaten straight up. For years if I didn't have at least a small supply of dark chocolate in the house, I felt anxious. Although I didn't eat an absurd amount of sweets, nevertheless they played an important part in my notion of a good life. You get the picture.

Then, I read several books that led me to give up refined sugar altogether, cold turkey. Enter the notion of a black-and-white decision. To my eyes, this behavioral approach means either going all in or getting all out, with no (or sparingly little) gray territory allowed. Although such a goal may sound extreme to you, and exceedingly difficult to pull off, below are some personal observations from using this powerful and empowering technique, some of which might surprise you.

I knew the only way I could handle giving up entirely on sweets was to treat it as an *experiment*. So, I committed to going sweets free but for only four weeks. By sweets free, I meant no refined sugar in all forms, including brown sugar, honey, maple syrup (which, as a native Vermonter, was especially hard to give up), agave nectar—you name it. Was this an easy change for me? Definitely not, especially at first. (It's true that whoever says change is easy is either crazy or lying.) But I managed to stay the course, and by the end of the month was rewarded with one of the biggest and most welcome surprises of my life: my craving for sugar was gone, completely gone. As if by magic, it had vanished.

At the end of that month, whenever a fellow staff member carried a tray of cookies or brownies back to the office kitchen where people could help themselves, I no longer heard the irresistible flute of the Sugar Pied Piper. Even dark chocolate had lost its grip on me. So, although I had initially declared the month of sweets free as an experiment, I quickly decided there was no way I was going back. Instead, I turned the delightful results of my experiment into a full-fledged habit, which I have stuck to firmly ever since.

The benefits of this change, thanks to my black-and-white decision, have been many. For one thing, I lost an easy seven or eight pounds—weight that has stayed off without effort. (Apparently, those were the "five pounds" I always felt I needed to lose, as I haven't had the thought since then.) My clothes fit better. I feel better physically. Plus, because I no longer had the taste of refined sugar to compare it to, I savored the natural sweetness of whole fruit as never before.

Over the course of my life I have made other black-and-white decisions. Thankfully on many levels, I quit smoking more than forty years ago. Every night *without exception* before going to bed I floss my teeth, even while camping in the wilderness. Another example is the time I kicked my diet cola habit. For many years, I drank one can of diet cola each day, a habit I fell in and out of over the years that always seduced me back. Because I'm highly sensitive to the effects of caffeine, missing even a single day of this habit brought on nervous energy, fitful sleep, and a debilitating headache from caffeine withdrawal. Only after I found a website for diet cola addicts did I name this habit for what it was—an addiction (if a modest one). I decided then and there to treat my decision as a black and white, to *never again* drink this beverage that was so bad for me. In that moment, which was well over ten years ago, I was finally able to quit for good.

What, then, are the biggest benefits of black-and–white decisions?

*1. A black-and-white decision frees up willpower.*

While writing this chapter, I listened to an interview with psychologist Roy F. Baumeister, co-author with science writer John Tierney of *Willpower: Rediscovering the Greatest Human Strength.* The authors liken human willpower to a muscle, which, like physical muscles, can only do so much work before fatigue sets in.

When people learn that I don't eat sweets, they frequently compliment me on my willpower. The irony, though, is that although during the initial month when I gave up sweets I did indeed expend a great deal of willpower, but when my experiment morphed into a habit it no longer took much, if any, willpower, to sustain. I can gaze on a table of desserts purely out of curiosity, without being tempted a whit to put any of them into my mouth. With one big decision and choice, I've eliminated a lot of smaller ones that could easily pull me off course. In other words, I don't have to spend a shred of willpower on not eating sweets. How sweet is that?

*2. Over time, a black-and-white decision becomes second nature, simply part of who you are.*

I can't recall exactly when it happened, but at one point after giving up refined sugar I realized that I was a true "convert," that I simply can't imagine myself ever resuming my old habits.

In *Changing for Good: A Revolutionary Six-Stage Program for Overcoming Bad Habits and Moving Your Life Positively Forward* by James O. Prochaska et al., the authors outline stages of change based on studies of successful changers. They identify a final stage of change they call *termination*, which means the person has resolved the issue, with no chance of relapse. (Prochaska, 274-280)

However, given what we know about human behavior, such a stage seems difficult, if not impossible, to achieve 100 percent of the time. To illustrate, I offer a different example of a faithful habit in my life, but one that defies the level of pure black and white. On every day but Sunday, I have a decades-long, firm commitment to exercise almost immediately after getting out of bed. But sometimes circumstances make this an impossible goal to meet. When this happens, though, which is not often, I can feel, almost viscerally, how much more willpower I must spend to resume my routine after a lapse of only a single day.

That said, in my habit of not eating refined sugar I believe I have achieved the termination stage of change. The main element that undergirds this firm feeling is, I believe, the black-and-white nature of that decision. Although I assiduously steer clear of processed foods (which often include sugar as an ingredient), eating traces of sugar in this society is inevitable and not something I fret about. That said, I have not eaten a single dessert or piece of candy for more than ten years. In the same way, when I quit smoking, I knew viscerally that I could never again put even a single cigarette to my mouth. In the same way, I feel the danger in eating even a single piece of candy. So, I simply don't do it.

Is the black-and-white criterion appropriate for all decisions? Not in the least. Like everyone else, I have my indulgences. When it comes to food, for me eating potato chips is a good example. Can I imagine life without potato chips? No, I can't. When I tell my story about giving up sweets, I'm not standing on a soapbox telling others to do the same. Nobody listens to that sort of speech anyway. The truth is that when I tell people my story, usually they look at me like I'm crazy. My favorite reaction was from a friend of mine who shot me a look of amazement and asked, incredulously, "Why ever would you do *that*? You know, you're not going to *be here* all that long!" In reply, I laughed long and loud.

Still, I hope you'll take time to mull over the power of making a black-and-white decision and where you might consider applying it in your life. You'll find great power waiting to be tapped. Bowl of fresh strawberries anyone (hold the sugar)?

*Postscript.* In this chapter, I do not intend in any way to downplay how fraught with complications food issues can be and often are. People are not all alike, and there is no single way to achieve good health, as we individually define it.

## *Questions to Ponder*

- Can you think of one black-and-white decision you've already made in your life?
- Is there a relatively small troublesome activity or habit you might like to consider changing with a black-and-white decision?
- Is there a larger "experiment" you might eventually want to undertake at some point (along the lines of my experiment in giving up sweets)? If so, what are some smaller steps you might take leading up to it?

VI

# Take Care

A RITUAL THAT rubs me the wrong way, despite it being well-intended, is to say to kids (or anybody else) as they're about the walk out the door, "Be careful." This advice seems to be rooted in a belief that life is dangerous in a pervasive way, even if there is no immediate threat apparent, and that, therefore, we must always be on our guard, be on the defensive. (I completely understand cautioning someone to be careful when they're on the verge of engaging in an activity that may be fraught with actual risk or danger.)

An alternative that has worked better with me is, "Take care." In general, this phrase is seen as a shorthand version of, "take care of yourself," which, in contrast to *be careful,* is spoken primarily as an expression of caring, as in, "You're important to me; please take care of yourself."

I have entitled this section *Take Care* because so many people, based on my observations, spend far less energy than they could or should on taking care of themselves. I also believe that taking care of ourselves is not, by itself, a selfish act, for when we take care of ourselves, we also become better able to take care of others.

You'll find chapters here that touch on a range of such *taking care* activities as walking, getaways, handling down moods, seeking medical care, and reframing painful memories.

CHAPTER 36

# Take Time for Getaways

A FEW WINTERS ago, my husband and I drove north to spend two nights at a B&B in Prudenville, Michigan for some cross-country skiing or snowshoeing and for some time together away from never-ending lists of household and life chores.

The room the innkeepers assigned to us was lovely, with green walls the color of moss on cedar, a plush, fabric-covered loveseat in front of a gas fireplace, and ivory-colored bedroom furniture that included a tall four-poster bed with a collection of soft pillows. Tucked in a corner of the room a covered hot tub, surrounded by two sections of knotty-pine wainscoting, called to us.

On the table next to my side of the bed, I found a spiral-bound journal made of fine quality paper. On top of it, at an angle, a pen beckoned to me. Inside the cover, our hosts had written: *Please share some thoughts about your stay with us.* Instantly curious, I carried the journal to the loveseat in front of the gas fireplace, which gave off a delicious warmth, and settled down to read. Like a magnet, each entry pulled me to the next one until I had devoured the entire journal, cover to cover. Later, I discovered two more such journals in the top drawer of the nightstand. Together, these three books told some of the stories about time spent inside these four walls during the previous ten years.

Some couples were here on their honeymoons (including, I was astonished to find, two close friends of ours who found each other later in life and married several years ago). Others came to celebrate anniversaries or special occasions. For some, their stay was a surprise arranged by a spouse or partner. Many people wrote about getting away from "reality"–demanding jobs, raising kids, and dealing with life's big and small problems and stresses, and of their dread at having to return to these things all too soon.

The more I read, the more grateful I felt that ever since our kids were old enough to leave in the care of their grandmother for a day or two, during more than forty years of marriage (and happily counting) my husband and have regularly made time for romantic getaways. (There are all kinds of getaways, of course, so the principle applies to everyone.) Although it's been many years since our younger daughter headed off to college and we had the house to ourselves most of the time, there we were that weekend, keeping alive the sweet tradition of our getaways.

I wish I could channel the timber and cadence of the many voices from the long line of couples who had come to this room before us and those who will arrive after us—the couples who have closed the drapes, at least for a day or two, on the rest of their lives and who have let the minutes and hours expand into the kind of space it's so difficult to find and even harder to give ourselves. (Not to worry; even with my journal reading there was plenty of time for romance during our stay in that beautiful room.)

A slogan from Louis Vuitton in the 1920s declared, "Show me your luggage and I'll tell you who you are." Metaphorically, my memories from romantic getaways fill an oversized suitcase plastered with hotel luggage labels from a B&B near Arcadia National Park in Maine to an archetypally romantic cabin at Strathcona Park Lodge in the middle of Vancouver Island, British Columbia, and lots of lovely places in between. But these labels can only hint at the countless moments of simply being together as, thread by thread, my husband and I have continued to weave the tapestry of an ever-deeper friendship and a long, fulfilling marriage.

Early one morning a few days ago, while still contemplating the quiet power of getaways, I drove the short distance from our house into town at just the time of morning when lots of people are in a mad dash to get to work. In the span of less than a minute, as I approached side streets to my right, one by one three different drivers, all of them in a rush, jerked their cars to sudden stops, well past the white line that indicates where, by law, drivers are supposed to stop. Their cars were far enough into the intersection, and close enough to my car, to have triggered in me a fight-or-flight reaction, as my heart raced and my eyes widened in fear.

Because so many of us are in a head-spinning rush to be somewhere else, this kind of thing is happening more and more, and, with it, mounting stress on our bodies and minds and the all too real potential for injury or worse. (And then there are the crazies on the freeway who dart in and out of lanes to gain another twenty or thirty feet–as if it were all a video game where bodies aren't made of flesh and blood and where fiery accidents are merely a signal to boot up a new game.)

*Yes,* I thought to myself, as I drove into town. *In this busy, crazy world, getaways are more important than ever, whether as a gift to one's self or with a friend or partner.* As we swim upstream against the achievement-drunk culture that surrounds us, too often we let the trappings of our many responsibilities, big and small, drown out who we are at the core. Life is too precious and short not to occasionally take a break from our obsession with *doing* to give ourselves some time and space to just *being.*

If the kind of getaway described here is financially out of reach, there are simpler, inexpensive alternatives. Make a date for a walk in a park. Pack a simple lunch and enjoy a picnic next to a river, preferably near the soothing sounds of a waterfall (even a small one—what matters is the soothing sound of water over rocks) or a lake. Or create an evening picnic on your living room floor, with lit candles and soothing background music. (If you purchase a colorful tablecloth to use only for such occasions, it will signal you that it's time to get away.) Take turns planning a simple outing, such as visiting a museum and going out afterward for coffee or a glass of wine. Check out free local concerts, and make a firm date to attend one. To make it more fun, take turns with the planning and make it a surprise. Although stays at a B&B are nice, the most important element of a getaway, regardless of its size, is to break out of your usual routine.

Now if you'll excuse me, I must pick up the phone to make a reservation for our next getaway. After my hair-raising drive into town, I'll tell the B&B owners, "Instead of two nights, make it three."

## *Questions to Ponder*

- When was the last time you gave yourself (or you and your partner) a getaway?
- If you tell yourself such a trip just isn't possible (e.g., due to limited funds or what feels like never enough time), what are some alternative, creative ways to design a getaway?
- Who else in your life could help you make it happen?
- What would it take for you to make it happen?
- If not now, when?

CHAPTER 37

# Walk Proud

AS MENTIONED EARLIER, in the late 1970s, while Rick and I were living in Eugene, Oregon, I caught the running bug. I ran faithfully until a sad day when, following damage to a ligament in my right knee from an injury ten years earlier that I had foolishly ignored, the last small shred of cartilage in my right knee wore down almost to bone and stopped me dead in my tracks.

During my running years, three times each week, year-round and in all kinds of weather, I faithfully tied the laces of my running shoes and headed out the door to put in my three miles. While some people run in an obligatory response to an inner *should*, I *loved* everything about running: being outdoors in all kinds of weather, the rhythm of my legs pumping up and down, the sound of my breathing, the ebb and flow of morning light over the course of a year, and feeling my feet hit the ground stride after stride. I also liked the identity of being a runner, which I carried proudly.

So, when my injured knee forced me to give up running, I dove into a period of deep grief. Before long, though, my long-standing commitment to regular exercise turned my head toward biking, a much kinder exercise for my bum knee. After I brought home a high quality, stationary exercise bike, my morning runs gave way to three thirty-minute, high-revolution, low-resistance, heart-pumping rides per week. It's a routine I follow to this day. But since spending time outdoors is a key ingredient in my recipe for wellbeing, and because weight-bearing exercise is important for strong bones and I plan to stay active and strong for decades to come, I also became a faithful walker.

Over the years, I began to envy runners less and to love walking more–in some ways even more than running.

For one thing, walking is quieter and more tranquil. Also, I sometimes walk on trails in the woods, which, with their roots, rocks, and occasional short stumps that jut out of impacted earth, I was too cautious to run on. Walking also gives me time and space to pay attention to–and often savor—such things as the parade of spring flowers, the texture of the river changed by shifting breezes and winds, and the canopy overhead, luscious green in summer and crisscrossed in winter with thick and heavy branches and gossamer-thin twigs.

What makes me sad, though, is the many people who *don't* walk regularly, or even occasionally. When I'm out walking on blue-sky days in spring, the kind lovers of the outdoors wait for all winter long, I puzzle over why I'm not surrounded by people who are also out to enjoy the day. When it comes to exercise, I worry that in many people's minds running has wrongfully staked its claim as being the *best* exercise and perhaps even as the only *real* exercise. Not true!

Plus, there's the cool factor, which also worries me. Running has evolved into a decidedly cool sport. Just watch any group of two or three runners waiting at a traffic light to cross the street–hands on hips, jogging in place, or stretching. Now compare them to a small group of people out for a walk, standing there, without fanfare, waiting to cross the street. Walking is boring. Running is cool. Again, I say, not true!

I think the glamour we ascribe to running is a great disservice to most people. My passion for walking was emboldened by a playful and information-packed YouTube video by Dr. Mike Evans, a physician who, with a team of people, creates online whiteboard lectures to promote good health habits. His lecture *23½ Hours: What Is the Single Most Important Thing We Can Do for Our Health?* had a big impact on me. (As you might guess, the missing half hour is reserved for exercise, with *walking* spelled out in clear terms as a fabulous choice.) In the lecture, Dr. Evans paints a picture (literally) of the enormous benefits of being even minimally active and the all-too-real dangers of being sedentary. Watching the video shifted my thinking and made me feel *proud* to be a walker.

So, if you're a runner, good for you. But if you're one of the millions more who, despite good intentions, don't exercise regularly, I propose that you begin to see walking as both a fun and *cool* option for staying active. Below are the main reasons why.

*1. Almost everyone can walk.*
Not everyone can run, not by a long shot. As to whether everyone who runs *should* run is a different question. Although running can be great exercise for people of all builds, we've all seen runners who look like they're about to either have a massive heart attack or seriously hurt themselves, and who make us want to beg them to stop.

*2. Walking, especially brisk walking, gives all the benefits of exercise without the risk of stressing or injuring the body.*
Our bodies are perfectly designed for walking. The benefits we accrue from a regular regimen can include better blood circulation, cardiovascular fitness, and more energy. Regular walking can also help us to prevent or address such health risks as high cholesterol (the bad kind), high blood pressure, and the risk of heart attack or stroke.

*3. Walking is free.*
No gym or personal trainer membership required.

*4. Walking is convenient.*
If you're like most people, to take a walk all you need to do is head out the door (or drive a short distance to a place with good walking options, be it a park or a neighborhood).

*5. It's generally easy to find a friend to walk with.*
Since almost everyone can walk, it's likely you can find someone who's not just willing to but would love to join you. (He or she will probably even thank you for suggesting it.) Evidence shows that we're more likely to stick with it when we have an exercise partner.

*6. The more relaxed pace of walking lets us enjoy our surroundings.*
Whether it's houses in a neighborhood, the sky, trees, or people we pass, walking (more than running) gives us time to check out this glorious world we live in at a more leisurely pace. Before I retired in 2011 from a long career as an administrator in higher education, for lots of good reasons I followed a long-standing practice of getting outside every day for at least a short walk, which I'm incredibly glad I made a habit. Walking in a natural setting such as a park is even more of a treat.

*7. Walking is the perfect life-long exercise.*
As they age, at some point most runners will need to trade in their running shoes for something else. I know from experience how hard this is to do. But walking is an exercise option that most people can continue to do for their entire lives. Walking is like a dependable, loyal friend who will always be there for you.

One time while driving east to New York on Route 80, I chuckled when I saw a public service sign that advised, tongue in cheek, "Buckle up for the next million miles." If you've been scolding yourself that you *should* join the gym, start running, lose weight, etc., you might want to imagine a sign just inside your front door that reads, "Put on your walking shoes for the next million steps." (Realistically, for most people this equates to less than five hundred miles–an easily achievable goal over a lifetime.) Plus, don't forget to put on your sunglasses and add a little swagger to your walk. Walk proud, I say.

In my mind, I picture you up ahead on a walking path. As we walk toward each other, I stop, spread my arms wide, and say, borrowing Billy Crystal's Cheshire Cat grin as well as his famous words, "You look *mah-ve-lous!*" So, you do, cool walker you.

## *Questions to Ponder*

- Are you holding yourself to any difficult, perhaps impossible goals for exercise?
- What's one way you could be fairer to yourself?
- Where is your favorite nearby place to take walks?
- What's one simple way you could increase the amount of walking you do?
- Does the name of a friend come to mind who might welcome the chance to walk with you, even occasionally?
- What activities might you be willing to forego to walk for a half hour instead?

## CHAPTER 38

# Treat Your Body Like the Friend It Is

One morning, I had a stomachache. Nothing big. It didn't keep me from riding my stationary bike, eating breakfast, or doing other parts of my morning routine. It was simply my body talking to me again in an old conversation about eating certain foods that are bad for me, especially wheat.

What had brought on this discomfort? On the previous day, over lunch with a good friend, I ordered lentil soup. When the man behind the deli counter asked if I wanted bread (typically a large end of the rye bread the restaurant slices up for sandwiches), my body answered with a firm no. But then, in a split second, I ignored my own best advice, and said yes to the bread. Between sips of hot, comforting soup, I relished every bite of that bread, spread generously with butter, knowing full well I would pay a price. The next day, there I sat, with a disgruntled stomach.

Of all foods, wheat upsets my stomach most. Or it could be the gluten in the wheat; being self-diagnosed, I'm not sure. The story of how I discovered this intolerance goes back more than ten years to a family Thanksgiving celebration in New Jersey. For years, I had suffered from stomachaches, with no clear cause. On that Thanksgiving Day, I stumbled like a clumsy scientist onto the reason for them. Just that morning my husband had kindly driven to a pharmacy to buy me a bottle of round, pastel-colored antacid tablets. Because I hardheadedly resist using medication, I was trying antacid for the first time. After eating far too much for dinner, which included a large helping of stuffing, some dinner rolls, and a large piece of pie (in other words, plenty of wheat), I felt awful. The antacid seemed to have had no effect whatsoever. As I reclined on the sofa, rubbing my belly, in a flash the truth hit me like a bolt out of the blue. As I slapped my hand to my forehead, I said out loud, more to myself than anyone near me, "It's the bread!" (Or the wheat in it.) As lessons go, it was a banner day.

In the coming days, during which I ate no bread or wheat-based foods whatsoever, my guess proved to be worthy. So, ever since, I've mostly stayed away from it. But there are times even today, many years later, when I give in to temptation, when I ignore my better judgment. Returning to that morning after lunch with my friend, the reality of my choices the day before glared at me, crossing its arms in disdain. Although this wasn't a new dance, on that day I received a bit of wisdom as if it had been written on a scrap of paper and passed to me in class.

All in all, I treat my body well: healthy, balanced eating; home-cooked meals; virtually no sweets; a decades-long commitment to strength and aerobic workouts; almost daily walks; and an active lifestyle. When responding to the litany of questions my doctor asks during my annual wellness exam, my answers make her happy. All in all, I'm on a solid foundation for good health. The year I first wrote this chapter I turned the age made famous by the Beatles' tongue-in-cheek reference to needing and feeding. With healthy habits and life expectancy tables on my side, I hope to be around for at least another twenty years.

But that morning, as I felt the aftereffects of eating a large portion of bread a day earlier, it came to me that it might not be quite as simple (or carefree) as waiting for the ache in my stomach to pass. *Might,* I asked myself, *there be some damage left behind when the loyal army of cells in my digestive tract once again miraculously returns me to feeling well? Was I being foolish to assume the penalty was short-lived, here and then gone again?* Suddenly I was not so sure.

That morning, as my stomachache thankfully began to fade, I received not one but two lessons. The first was that when I eat a sizable portion of bread, I indulge myself in immediate gratification, and turn my back on the inevitable (if delayed) consequence of feeling physically lousy. *After all,* I tended to tell myself, *my stomach doesn't hurt while I'm eating.* When I give in to such emotion-based desire, I make the same shortsighted trade people everywhere make far too often: immediate, short-term gratification over long-term wellbeing.

That day, while writing, as I contemplated my weakness in the face of delicious bread, what didn't jibe was the decision I had made years earlier, when I gave up eating sweets, up one of life's cross-cultural elixirs. How had I managed to make such a difficult sacrifice, which for most people is out of the question–no way, no how, unh uh, not happening? One thing that helped me make that big change was to have learned in detail what happens in the body when we feed it a sudden surge of sugar. The wild blood sugar and hormonal swings that follow are akin to riding in a car that careens down the road, tires screeching, as the threat of a rollover floods the brain. When it comes to not eating refined sugar, many years ago I made a firm decision, one I have been fiercely loyal to it ever since: I will not do this to my body! As I was writing, I wondered whether I could use the same determination when it came to eating wheat-based foods.

So why, with that victory notch on my belt, was I continuing to surrender to the temptation of bread? Thinking about this led me to a second lesson. I realized the story I had been telling myself about what was happening inside my body when I eat wheat bordered on dishonest. When I treated my body like foe rather than friend, what was the true casualty count? When I tore off a bite of bread with my teeth, I was as good as going to war with this forgiving body of mine, even if at first the battlefield seemed deceptively quiet (since it takes time for my digestive system to react). But without a doubt what I had been doing at such times was going into battle against *myself.*

In her book *The Autoimmune Solution,* Amy Myers has described how gluten intolerance plays out in the body, as described briefly below. (By referring to Dr. Myers's book, my intention is not to endorse the system she puts forth in its pages.)

- The gut encounters unfamiliar proteins that are created in wheat when it's hybridized (to help it grow faster and to resist drought and bugs). (Myers, 102.)

- In the presence of these unfamiliar proteins, our bodies produce antibodies that attack gliadin, one of the two peptides found in gluten. (Myers, 94.)
- Over time the blanket of microvilli in our gut (which absorb nutrients) becomes less effective. (Myers 75, 97.)
- As wheat has become more prevalent in the food we eat and has also been made more water-soluble, these negative effects in the body happen more and more frequently. (Myers, 102-103.)

For me, Dr. Myers' description of what takes place in the gut painted a much clearer picture of the war I wage on myself when I eat wheat-based foods. With each passing year, this war within has contrasted ever more sharply with the deepening gratitude I feel each and every day simply to be alive. Such moments have included gliding along almost effortlessly in a set of cross-country ski tracks deep in the woods when I suddenly began to weep, or a day when I sat drinking tea while seated at the small glass-topped table for two in a corner of our kitchen in the Pontiac Trail house, as the warmth of the sun on my back flooded me with an almost overwhelming sense of good fortune.

One of the reasons I have remained so firmly committed to not eating refined sugar is that I truly believe it brings me better health and, along with it, more days to relish being alive. As I thought about the ways I had treated my body like an enemy by consuming bread and other foods that are not good for me, I began to hope that the more honest description of what I was doing to my body at such times (i.e., waging war within) could help me, in moments of temptation, to remember that my body is not the enemy but rather the most loyal of comrades. In that moment, I made a commitment to stand side by side *with* my body, to work in concert with it, as I say a big *yes* to life itself.

## *Questions to Ponder*

- At times, most of us wage war on our bodies. What's one way you do this?
- What would it take for you to tip the scales away from choices that hurt you toward choices that help?
- What are the ways you're being good to your body? What's one thing you could do to be even better for it?

CHAPTER 39

# Lessons from My Mother's Cancer

THROUGHOUT MY LIFE, I have puzzled over why all my precious few memories of my mother are so negative. One example is the time I was playing in the bathtub and called out to her. When she didn't come, and didn't come, I wrapped myself in a towel and marched matter-of-factly, eyes straight ahead, out the front door. Mom, it turns out, was there all along, leaning into the open window on the passenger side of a car pulled up in front of our house, engrossed in conversation with a friend.

The most painful of these heavy-hearted memories was from a day about two years later. My brother Peter and I had climbed into the backseat of the family's baby blue Dodge Lark to join our parents as they ran some errands. With the windows rolled partway down to let in some of the warm spring air, we bounced up and down on the backseat. After my mother, who never learned to drive, climbed into the front passenger seat in front of me, spontaneously I stood up, leaned into the front seat, and threw my arms around her in a big hug. When Mom cried out suddenly in pain, I quickly released my grip and sat back on the seat, scared and afraid I had done something terribly wrong. With sharpness in his voice I had never heard before, my father turned to her and said, "That's it!" As he shifted the car into gear and turned around to look behind him as he backed into the road he added, "You have *got* to go to the doctor." Later, I realized, this incident was the first signal that something was wrong with our mother, something very wrong. There was another never-before event as we drove into town: No one said another word.

Another vivid childhood memory was when my mother was recovering from the removal of one of her breasts. After I begged her several times to show me the scar, and perhaps because we were the only girls in the house, she eventually gave in. For privacy, she led me by the hand to the corner of the room just behind the door, where she lifted her blouse. My eyes traced the dark line where her right breast had been. When I asked if I could touch it, she nodded. My fingers gently touched the small bumps left by the stitches. Thrilled to be invited into this circle with her, and blind to what was to come, I felt special to have been brought into this dark secret. Not long afterward came the surgery to remove her other breast.

The cruel march of Mom's decline brings to my mind another, especially lucid memory. Although only much later would we kids come to understand the progression of Mom's cancer and its effects, after the cancer spread to Mom's brain she became increasingly incoherent. For this reason and to protect us from seeing more than my father thought was wise, more and more often the door to our parents' bedroom was closed. One day, I recall, my brother and I went in to visit her. While we were there, when Mom reached for the glass of water sitting on a chair next to the bed, she tipped it over, spilling water on the chair and floor. Her voice filled with despair, she cried out, "Oh, now look at what I've done–knocked over the jar of peanut butter again!"

My brother and I looked at each other. *Peanut butter? She thinks the water is peanut butter?* Since kids will be kids even when their mother is dying, and since no one had explained to us at that point the reason behind her confusion, we began to giggle. Before our laughter could grow into a full-blown guffaw, as our father called it, we rushed out of the room, almost slamming the door behind us. Bursting into one of the other bedrooms, we threw ourselves onto the bed, bent over in huge belly laughs. Later, it would be a scene we would have a hard time forgiving ourselves for, even though, as kids, we hadn't done anything wrong.

A final memory was from the day I rushed into the house after a car ride my father took my brothers and me on to break the news to us that Mom was dying. With the enthusiasm of a nine-year-old kid who had no idea what was about to hit her, and the ways it would affect her for the rest of her life, after we arrived back home I rushed into the house to where our grandparents, who had been staying with us, sat gravely at the kitchen table, feeling the weight of the difficult errand their son was on. Cheerfully, I announced, "Our mother is dying, and afterward we might get a new house!" With tears in her eyes, my grandmother drew me into her arms for a long, tight hug.

As it turned out, Mom died the very next night, while we kids were in the middle of watching the *Wizard of Oz*. (Since our mother was also a Dorothy, later I imagined she, too, clicked her ruby red slippers together three times.) As clearly as if it were yesterday, I see myself leaning against my father, his eyes red, tears falling down his face as he told us Mom had died. It was the first time I saw him cry. We kids were shuffled next door to Mrs. Morse's house, where we sat on the sofa, staring silently through her large picture window at the ambulance parked in our driveway, there to carry away our mother.

Over time I have found two important lessons embedded in these painful memories. The first is a knowledge that I remember these painful experiences so clearly because the reptilian part of the brain tends to store memories of threat and danger for easy recall, to enhance our chances of survival.

But at the same time, I now see, without a doubt, that many positive memories (the kind I have always hungered for) are lodged somewhere in the recesses of my mind, even though I can't ferry them to consciousness. This knowledge has gradually led me to believe, without a doubt, that our mother, who was known for her gentle, loving ways and playful laugh (people told us she never had a bad word to say about anybody), must have spent many happy hours with me on her lap or in her arms, or caressing the top of my head when I rushed up for a hug. Since, in addition, our happier memories tend to simply fade into the backdrop of our lives, I was also simply too young when Mom died to store those memories in a place where I could find them later. The first lesson, then, is that even though I can't recall those many wonderful memories, they happened.

The second lesson I have taken is how important it is to act without delay in the face of any health concern. We later learned from Dad that when our mother first found the lump in her breast, she was too scared to tell anyone, including him. For months, she carried it like a small but heavy stone in not just her breast but in her heart. Even after coming out with the truth to our father, she pleaded with him not to make her see a doctor, not just yet. For unknown reasons, he gave in to her pleading, until that day in the car when I hugged her. It's quite possible that when her fingers found the first lump it was already too late. But what we knew back then and still know today is the most effective treatment for cancer is, wherever possible, to remove it surgically. By waiting, Mom almost certainly cast her fate.

What would our lives have been like if she had found the courage to do otherwise? How would I, and my life, be different if she had lived to see her children grow up and hold her grandchildren in her arms? I will never know, of course. But by sharing these stories with you, I am asking you, indeed, pleading with you: If you sense something might be wrong with you physically, please don't second-guess yourself. Please don't wait. If you love life, and I hope you do, pick up the phone. Make the appointment. Do it now.

## *Questions to Ponder*

- Can you think of any positive memories buried somewhere in your mind that would help to counter the negative memories you vividly recall?
- Can you think of a negative memory that might have a positive side for you?
- In which ways do you most love life?
- Are there any potential health concerns you're choosing to ignore or keep silent about? What powerful, positive reasons might help you to act now?

## CHAPTER 40

# Listen to the Voice Within

As I WROTE this chapter, an incision on my lower right back, marked by a neat row of straight black stitches, was healing day by day. The doctor had ordered me to take it easy (What? Who? Me?), which meant, in part, no exercise. So, on that Saturday morning, I sat in front of our gas fireplace instead of doing my typical Saturday morning workout and then my weekly trip to the farmer's market. While part of me felt a bit sorry for myself, mostly I felt grateful. This is a story that may be about attention, intuition, good plain luck … or about something much more mundane.

Six weeks earlier, while walking with a good friend, she happened to mention a visit to a dermatologist for what she described as a full skin scan. As she spoke these words, a voice within me said clearly and distinctly, *you need to do that … now!* (I had never undergone such a scan.) As luck would have it, less than a week later I visited my doctor for an annual exam scheduled a full year in advance. Pointing to a spot near my naval, which was small and symmetrical (a good sign) but whose dark color concerned me, I asked my doctor for a referral to a dermatologist, which she promptly agreed to do.

Less than two weeks later, I drove to the appointment. As a medical resident looked over every inch of my skin, she said she wasn't concerned at all about the dark spot I had been worried about, nor about the small fields of seborrheic keratosis (harmless skin patches) that crop up on various parts on my body, especially my back. But during the exam, as she dwelled on an area of my lower back she paused and then asked, "Did you know you have a mole here?" When I said I was unaware of it, she added, "I don't like the way it looks." After the attending doctor, based on her follow-up exam, agreed with the resident's concern, by the time I walked out the door less than thirty minutes later, that mole was a test tube on the way to pathology.

A week later, the resident called to tell me in a reassuringly cheery tone of voice that the pathology report showed no signs of melanoma (I'm sure you can imagine my huge sigh of relief.). Since she sounded so lighthearted, I assumed this meant I was in the clear. But then, after a pause, she added *the pathologists did, however, find highly unusual cells.* As someone whose mother was killed by cancer, her words send me into a small-scale panic. Four days later, I returned for a procedure to remove a larger section of the skin surrounding the mole. As is often true, my dread beforehand was far worse than the procedure itself. After a series of small pricks (from the numbing shots), I felt nothing while the doctor performed the surgery, other than a sense of tugging as she sewed in the stitches.

A few weeks later my life returned to its usual rhythms, and the scar from the incision, while it may never disappear entirely, has already faded. During the days after the surgery, I spent lots of time imagining what might have happened if that series of domino events—walking with my friend, following up on my inner nudge, and the medical treatments that followed–had not unfolded. *What was it*, I asked myself, *that pushed over the first domino? What prompted the voice within? Intuition? Did I know at some level that this part of my body needed attention? Or was it just serendipity or old-fashioned luck?*

Perhaps my intuition, as I tend to think of it, is nothing more than the illusion of causation, the tendency to see a relationship between two overlapping events where, in fact, no such connection exists. On the other hand, I've always seen myself as an intuitive person, even if I don't always *act* on my inner nudges. So, despite being aware of this type of illusion, I still choose to believe that in the case of the mole on my back, my intuition–with its inner warning chime—did me a favor.

But perhaps an even more basic lesson is how important it is for us to pay attention to our skin. If you're a Baby Boomer like me, you, too, may have spent long afternoons as a teenager lying on a beach towel on the hard concrete that surrounded the public pool, lathered in baby oil, which (to no one's surprise, as we later became aware) offers zero protection against the sun's harmful rays. At the time, all my friends and I cared about was turning our pale skin into a deep bronze that, unbeknownst to us, first became a symbol of affluence among the well-to-do but then gradually worked its way down through the social classes to people like me and my friends, and blue-collar kids like us all over the country.

So, here's to waking up to both the illusions of life that many of us would be surprised to learn are our daily fare, and at the same time to listening to and acting on our inner wisdom. But even if all you hear within is a deafening silence, pure and simple here's to taking care of your skin, possibly with some help from your doctor. Now please pass the sunscreen—and, while you're at it, that rather silly-looking, broad-brimmed hat that helps keep skin safe and, quite possibly, also keeps skin cancer at bay.

## *Questions to Ponder*

- Are there any inner nudges that won't leave you alone? What might they be about? Are you being called in some way toward action or change?
- Are there ways you want to take care of yourself (without or within) but tend not to? What's one thing that could help you to move in that direction?

CHAPTER 41

# Trading in My Cloak of December Blues

ONE NIGHT SEVERAL years ago in early December, when I was in an especially down mood, my husband reminded me I was in my blue time of year. As I thanked him for reminding me, a picture came to mind of myself slipping my arms into the sleeves of an imagery cloak and then pulling it on, this self-woven cloak of December blues. As compared to a coat, a cloak is long, with a hood—a piece of clothing that tends to envelope its wearer. I know the main reasons why the last month of the year is a tough one for me emotionally.

First and foremost, both of my parents died in December. The number of years they've been gone astonishes me (when this book is published, it will have been fifty-seven years for Mom and thirty-three years for Dad). This chapter is about a time a few years ago when I received a long overdue wake-up call to trade in my cloak of blues for a new garment, one that helps me weather this hard time of year. (As you read this, I invite you to think about any unhelpful cloaks currently hanging in your closet that you may want to consider trading in.)

The second main source of my annual December blues was a collection of vividly sad memories from Decembers past that would rush back to me each year to weave the annual sense of melancholy I wore for most of the month. The first of those memories was from the December when Mom died.

Less than a week after burying Mom, my father drove my three brothers and me the seven hours to Newfield, New York, for a long holiday weekend with my Uncle Kendall (my mother's only sibling), my Aunt Louise, and my cousin Richie. What I remember most about that trip was a few hours of great joy that, as I matured, morphed into a memory laced with guilt. Waking up that year on Christmas morning sometime before five a.m., my cousin and I raced downstairs to dump out the contents of our Christmas stockings on the living room rug, where we found whirling, twirling, metal noisemakers that my aunt and uncle, lying in their warm bed, must have instantly cursed themselves for buying.

For the next hour or two, we ran like banshees around the downstairs loop—the kind of loop every house with kids in it should have—from kitchen to dining room to living room, around and around. Twirling those noisemakers with abandon, we laughed ourselves to the point of exhaustion. As I grew older, though, my view of that jollity considerably darkened as I pictured my father, listening to our racket, lying terribly alone in his bed as he woke up to another day of feeling the empty place next to him on the bed, knowing, in his mind if not in his heart, that my mother would never again lie next to him. Looking back, I felt increasingly ashamed of my cousin's and my tomfoolery, especially so soon after my mother's death and even if our rambunctiousness, unbeknownst to us, offered a kind of salve for the sadness that suffused Christmas that year.

Another painful memory has stayed with me, this one from a series of largely joyless Christmases after my father remarried. In December of the year I turned nineteen, I was full of existential angst and questions about God and life. In such a state, I was adamant about not going with the rest of the family to attend Christmas Eve services. As soon as my father backed the car out of the driveway, I switched off the ubiquitous television, flooding the room with the sweet quiet I had been craving all day. I sat alone in front of the sterile aluminum tree my stepmother had purchased years earlier to avoid the mess of a real tree. (My own mother hated fake flowers and would, I believe, have also hated what I found to be a glittering sham of a Christmas tree.) Near the tree, a four-section color wheel pointed up at it, whirring softly, turning the tree's icicle-like branches by turns red, yellow, blue, and green. It was close to midnight.

Next to the television that year sat a smug stack of boxes, each one covered in identical wrapping paper that defied personality, the kind of paper that comes with a free gift-wrapping service delivered with a yawn by underpaid young employees. My brother and I had concluded, correctly, that our father and stepmother must have done their holiday shopping that year at a sweater outlet. In their dullness, that stack of lifeless boxes, one of which I would unwrap the next morning as the sweater within took its place in a long line of disappointing gifts, dampened my already dark mood.

Yearning to be part of the type of happy Christmas scenes the media bombard us with before the holidays, tears trickled down my face. Being alone, I didn't bother wiping them away but let them drip down to my chin and onto my shirt. To hide my puffy eyes and, more importantly, my pain, I dragged myself to bed before the others came home.

In addition to my parents' deaths and this litany of sad Christmas memories, in the year of my wake-up call there was a new addition to my December blues. In late November that year, we had observed the first anniversary of my beloved mother-in-law's passing. When I had written the holiday shopping list that year, it was strange to leave off her name. But at the same time, it was at the very moment I sat, staring at my list, when my wake-up call showed up, unannounced. I could almost hear my mother-in-law's voice about how to walk away from what she called a pity party, which is just what it was. As something shifted inside, something big, I heard a long-overdue voice within sharing some excellent, much-needed advice.

*Stop. Enough. For heaven's sake, you're sixty-three years old. You've lived more than twenty years past the age when your mother died. Plus, if your parents were still alive today, they would be ninety-nine and ninety-eight—extreme outliers on any life expectancy table. Face it, my dear; you're now officially a member of the older generation with all its parts, bad and good. You have left far behind the adolescent fear that no one would ever love you, the exhaustion of being new parents, your kids' adolescent angst, and the years of feeling restless and vaguely unhappy in what was, by all outward signs, a terrific job. Plus, on the road ahead lies a measure of freedom that falls only to the fortunate, with choices galore. You've also dodged what you always feared—dying young like your mother. It is time, finally, to throw off the dark cloak you've been dragging out every year in early December. Who, after all, takes it out of the back of the closet year after year? You do, my dear. You.* With that, my mind ended its firm-handed but well-meaning lecture by adding, with a degree of gentleness: *Girl, just get over it.*

*Yes,* I said to myself. *Yes.* It *was* time to throw off my musty cloak of December blues. Thus, began a helpful dialogue within.

*Question*: What do you need to do to trade coats?
*Answer (within):* Just as with my coaching clients, I can draw on the rich metaphor before me—in this case, to "weave" myself a new cloak.

*Question:* At this time of year, what type of cloak would you prefer to pull on instead?
*Answer:* My new coat is luxuriously warm. It's also light, a pleasure to wear.

*Question:* What does it look like? Which color(s)? What type of fabric?
*Answer*: The same blend of royal blues and purples that fill my closet and jewelry box, woven of the softest of wool, blended with silk.

*Question:* When you slip your arms into its sleeves, how will it feel?
*Answer*: Divine—designed and tailored exactly for me.

*Question:* Instead of "Cloak of December Blues," what will you call this new coat? (This question feels like it's from a dear friend seated across the table.)
*Answer*: I will call it my *Joy in December* coat. Yes, that feels right. A coat rather than a cloak because it will be lighter and not cover my face and head. It will give me more breathing room and the chance to look all around me. Within, I gave myself over once more to the sound of it: *Joy in December.*

The new coat I imagined for myself would join another ritual that had been a source of some balm for my December blues, although not nearly enough to have much of a lasting effect. One of the fine Jewish traditions I have learned about from my husband and his side of the family is the annual ritual of lighting a twenty-four-hour memorial candle on the anniversary of a loved one's death (the Yahrtzeit). In addition to having lit such candles in memory of Rick's Dad and more recently for my mother-in-law, for many years I have also lit Yartzeit candles for my parents. On the second day of December I have annually lit such a candle for my father, and eleven days a candle for my mother. For each of them, I place a favorite photograph near where the candle burns. In the case of Mom, I place her candle on a small plate from the only set of nice dinner dishes she ever owned, bought piece by piece through a promotional offer at the grocery store where my parents did their weekly shopping. The dish design, surprisingly lovely for such a giveaway, is built around a small, delicate rose in the center of each piece. Placing her candle on one of her plates from so long ago gives me much pleasure. In some mystical way, it also calls forth a woman-to-woman bond I never got to experience because I was so young when she died.

In addition to burning Yahrtzeit candles in December, I found the idea of trading in my dark, heavy cloak of blues for a richly-colored Joy in December coat lifted my mood considerably and gave me a new sense of hope that I could finally turn things around. At the end of my inner dialogue, I told myself, as if I were my own coach at the end of a helpful session, *great work!* As I pictured myself donning my new Joy in December coat, I watched my inner self spin around in the mirror with a flourish and a smile. With the coat wrapped around me, I said to myself *it's about time*!

## *Questions to Ponder*

- Do you have a heavy or uncomfortable cloak you put on at times? What does it represent in how you live your life?
- What does it look like? Does it have a scent? How does it feel?
- What's one thing you could do to give yourself permission to stop wearing it, quite possibly to purge it from your closet?

- What type of coat would you rather wear, or would be good for you? What color would it be? How would it feel? What might you name it?
- What's one thing you can do to give yourself permission to choose the right coat(s) for you instead of simply wearing what's been hanging in your closet?

CHAPTER 42

# Nurture Your Inner Gardener

DURING EACH OF my visits with my daughter, son-in-law, and precious new grandson at their rented townhome in the Potrero Hill section of San Francisco, I took an early morning walk. During such a visit, one day I was having a largely inexplicable wrong-side-of-the-bed morning. After locking the door behind me, when I reached the bottom front step I turned right, up the steep section of deHaro Street where they lived. Due to my touchy mood, with each step my mind chewed fiercely away on a set of thoughts that had showed up an hour earlier out of nowhere, like bad friends I should have stopped hanging out with years ago but to whom I kept opening the door when they knocked.

Making my way uphill I followed one of the dirt paths that cuts through the Starr King Open Space, a plot of land left wild for animals, plants, and people. I appreciated my walks there on nearly every day of my visits, as well as the welcome relief that small piece of open land must have given to the people squeezed into the many rows of small houses that crowd together in the neighborhood. Glancing up, I took in the impressive sight of four tall trees on a hilltop that watched like sentinels over the comings and goings of people and their dogs. After a recent rain, everywhere except on the narrow, well-worn paths, small shoots of grass had pushed to the surface, hinting at the upcoming return of the much-awaited, lush green that typically covers the hills of San Francisco in February and March.

As my enemy thoughts hammered away, I reminded myself to breathe. *Deeply now,* I said to myself, *all the way to the bottom of your lungs. That's it. Fill up with fresh air. Slowly now, in and out, in and out. Ahh.* With my head a bit clearer, I walked the steep ups and deep downs of deHaro to where it intersects with Southern Heights, the high spot I climbed to on my first walk in the neighborhood—one that provides a sweeping, pulsing view of the building scape of downtown San Francisco, framed in by the narrow, jutting peak of the Transamerica Pyramid and the big, boxy, 52-story skyscraper named for where it sits at 555 California Street. I then cut over to Vermont Street and then Twentieth Street. Walking through the park there, I walked the wooden stairs down to the entrance of the Potrero Hill Community Garden. A sign next to the front gate reminded visitors this place was one of only a few unlocked community gardens in the city and asked for their help keeping the privilege alive by enjoying the garden *without* picking any of the flowers and produce grown here by the fifty-one people who were lucky enough to have been assigned a plot that year. One of the current gardeners, the placard said, was Lorraine Vinson, a founding gardener who had been cultivating food for thirty years on this land where goats once grazed.

I first discovered that particular community garden in the summer of 2013, when Rick and I felt, for the first time, the unparalleled bliss of holding a grandchild in our arms. During that two-week visit, we had many more chances to hold Jack and to help out in various ways during the transition of our son-in-law's return to work. Because my husband and I are early risers, on the first day of that visit and every day thereafter, we enjoyed the luxury of an early morning walk, marveling at the many beautiful succulents planted in pots or beds, along with a profusion of flowering trees (including many brilliantly colored bougainvillea). Our destination was one of our two favorite coffee shops, where Rick drank his freshly brewed coffee, I sipped my much less interesting herbal tea, and we both had lots of fun people watching the regulars and modern-day line of people stopping by to pick up a badly-needed coffee on their way to work.

Early one morning, just after the fog lifted to reveal yet another morning of bright sun shining down from a clear blue sky, Rick and I followed a route that brought us, for the first time, to the park and the adjacent community garden. Curious, I walked alone down to the garden and slowly, almost meditatively, stepped lightly along the narrow paths between the small beds. I especially admired a plot filled edge to edge with a profusion of dahlias in full bloom in a broad palate of colors: fuchsia, bright-eyed yellow, pure white, pale green, fire-engine red, deep wine, and more.

On that first visit, I tried to picture the women and men who tended those beds. While most people planted only vegetables, a few grew flowers only, which intrigued me. While many people were there to grow food, others planted for beauty, not just for themselves but for all who came to enjoy the garden. In the back of one bed, filled with vegetables, stood a pair of proud cornstalks, their tassels fine haired and unruly. In another plot, I was surprised to see, small fieldstones drew a diagonal line through the plot, creating triangles on either side filled with an impressive array of carefully arranged succulents. Because the stone path took up such valuable space, it seemed especially sweet … a statement of beauty, of sheer aesthetics.

On the day of my solo return to the garden, with my bad mood on the wane, I was sorry to find the dahlias were gone. Still, I enjoyed picturing those tubers, full of the promise of future blooms, pulled up from the dark earth and tucked away in dark closets, nestled into peat moss or some other organic material to keep them moist until being replanted in spring. I walked the garden as if it contained the secrets of a labyrinth. Some beds were fully cleared, covered with rich, chocolate-colored mulch. In others, hardy greens like kale and collards, still green and plush, prolonged the harvest. While gazing at a large, unfamiliar plant, I recognized its unripe flower as an artichoke, the first such plant I had laid eyes on.

Thinking back to the unhelpful thoughts that had earlier flooded my mind, I saw each of them as a small shoot in my inner garden bed. What do we cultivate in these inner gardens, yours and mine? The answer is an unfiltered, endless string of thoughts our mind produces, moment by moment. As gardeners of what are too often chaotic garden plots within, we tend to assume every seedling or plant (thought) is as important as the next, worthy of our attention. *Since I planted it,* we think, *it must be good*. But this is not true … and not helpful.

As inner gardeners, the most important tool we own is likely a hoe. All too often, our minds toss out seeds haphazardly, incoherently, and even, at times, spitefully, as if taking revenge against ourselves, or at least our peace of mind. *We do not need to fertilize these plants,* I say to myself. *We also can envision pulling them out!*

The garden bed in my mind stretched into the distance. Far behind me, distant plants (thoughts) have thankfully gone fallow (*Thank heavens,* I said to myself, shuddering to think what my life would have been like if my current garden bed (mind) included a lifetime of unhelpful thoughts). Before me, empty planting beds stretched into the distance. Looking down at my feet in this imaginary garden, I saw small fledging shoots of weeds that represented the unhelpful thoughts that had come to me earlier in the day. On my walk back home, I posed to myself some of the kinds of questions I ask my clients. What's the thought? How true is it? What affect is it having on you? How's that working? What thoughts would be kinder? What would a good friend across the table say to you about this? In my mind, I bent down in my mind garden to pluck the fledging shoots from the earth. As I pictured holding them in my open palm, I said out loud (being the only garden visitor that morning) *it's the compost bin for you.*

After I finished my walk, I took one last look at the Golden Gate Bridge in the distance, latched the gate behind me, and climbed the steps to the park, feeling a strong kinship with every keeper of that community garden. Much lighter in spirit, I imagined myself resting my inner gardener's hoe on my shoulder, began to whistle, and headed for home.

## *Questions to Ponder*

- Thinking about your own inner garden, do any thoughts or beliefs come to mind that grow there like troublesome weeds?
- Choosing one, what would it be like to dig it up and place it on the compost pile?
- What new thought or belief would you rather plant in your inner garden to take its place?
- If you were to picture in detail the hoe you could use to weed your inner garden, what would it look like?

## CHAPTER 43

# Keep the Yarn of Life Open and Loose

One day at our home on Pontiac Trail, I sat on the loveseat in the front room, where the sun streamed through the window as I knit row after long row of garter stitch on a sunflower-colored portion of a sweater for my grandson. When the yarn tangled suddenly (because I hadn't taken time before I began knitting to wind it into a ball), I grew exasperated. After finding the tail end of the skein, I began to pull out arm-lengths of yarn from its center, building a lattice-like pile of bright yellow yarn on my lap. However, when I reached the end of the yarn, where it attached to the sweater in progress, I realized my mistake and let out a groan.

The tail end of the yarn, which I needed access to, was at the very bottom of the pile of yarn on my lap. The method I had used to pull out the yarn from the skein was the exact opposite of where I should have begun (at the tail end of the unused yarn). As I took steps to remedy my mistake, I soon had a tangled mess on my hands. Since this wasn't the first time I had made this kind of mistake, I could see what lay ahead: a lot of painstaking and slow untangling, which reminded me of combing out snarls in my fine, freshly shampooed hair without having any conditioner on hand ... but much worse. As I sat back on the loveseat to stare down at the yarn, I sighed heavily before resuming my efforts.

Just then my husband walked into the room. Watching me work, he gently intervened, as he picked up the tangled mass of yarn and stretched it between his hands like a large Cat's Cradle. As I wound the yarn into a ball, he repeated occasionally, like a mantra, *keep it open and loose*. Whenever the yarn knotted itself, he told me to stop winding and then slowly drew the yarn further apart with his fingers. In an impressively short amount of time, I finished winding the yarn into a neat ball.

Before turning back to my knitting, I asked my husband, "Where did you learn to do that?" He shrugged and said, as he walked out of the room, "Just an old trick someone taught me to help untangle fishing line." The next morning, I continued to mull over his advice: *keep it open and loose.* What a rich metaphor! My mind then turned toward finding a way to apply this rule to something far more complicated than yarn: coping with moods and difficult emotions.

## *Up moods*

When we find ourselves in what I'll call an up mood (when life is looking good), we're more likely to be able to untie knots, real and metaphorical, with ease and confidence. Inner knots include such circumstances as learning you must complete a demanding task sooner than you thought, especially when you're already woefully short of time, or getting into an argument with your partner or spouse about a modest difference of opinion that seems to suddenly explode into possible grounds for divorce.

When we tackle such problems while being in an up mood, we hold the "yarn" in our hands with a natural looseness which improves our ability to untie knots. Plus, in an up mood we tend to encounter fewer "knots" or pay less attention to them when they happen. In an up mood, we ourselves are more open and loose, more able to undo the knots that come our way.

## *Down moods*

However, untying the knots of life while in a down mood, when we're often at our worst, is a different story. In a down mood, we perceive knots in the yarn of life as being worse than they actually are. In such a state, it's easy to think, *I'll never get this mess straightened out.* What actions can we take to do a better job of untangling life's knots? One approach could be to mentally bully oneself into being open and loose. But this idea ignores the reality of our ever-shifting patterns of mood: up and down, up and down. When I picture myself or anyone else trying to shame me into being open and loose, I imagine replying with an angry growl.

A far better approach is to consciously set aside, temporarily, the messy knots that we encounter while in a down mood, like putting one's "knitting" into a drawer to return to later. Then, as soon as you feel your mood begin to lift—when you'll be more naturally open and loose, you can take it out again. You'll almost certainly find that your improved mood helps you untie the knots with greater ease and skill. Plus, you may have avoided having created an even worse knot in your yarn of life by fighting with it while in a down mood. (Oh, the tangled emotional webs!)

Another way we can put this open and loose approach to good use is when dealing with anger or other destructive emotions. When we allow anger to get the best of us, we as much as yank on the yarn when it becomes tangled, thereby creating knots so small and tight as to seem beyond hope. Sometimes in a fit of anger, we say or do things that become the type of knots we may never be able to untangle completely. When we feel anger bubbling up within, we can take time to breathe deeply (a proven antidote to anger). We can also deliberately walk away from the situation at hand until we're in a better place to understand, explore, and address what lies beneath the destructive emotion that has us in its grasp.

By the way, in case you think my knitting metaphor is women's territory, it's not. In the earliest days of knitting, men predominated the craft, especially fishermen. And with today's resurgence in knitting, more and more men are taking up this relaxing, rewarding activity. So, in the face of life's inevitable knots that show up or that we manage to snarl for ourselves, the idea of being open and loose is decidedly gender neutral. To one and all, I wish you a life of good knitting (and untying knots) by keeping the yarn of your life open and loose.

## *Questions to Ponder*

- Can you think of one way you might you use the skill of keeping the yarn of your life open and loose?
- Can you think of a “knot” in your life you tied more tightly than you ever meant to? What’s one thing you could do to try to loosen it?
- Is there a knot in your life you want or need to untangle? In this situation, how might you use the approach of keeping it open and loose?

VII

# To Life!

"Dear old world," she murmured, "you are very lovely, and I am glad to be alive in you."

—L.M. Montgomery, *Anne of Green Gables*

Dost thou love life, then do not squander time, for that is the stuff life is made of.

—Benjamin Franklin, *Poor Richard*

CHAPTER 44

# Lessons from My Newborn Grandson

On the first Sunday in August 2013, my husband and I settled into our seat on Flight 457 from San Francisco to Phoenix and then home to Michigan after spending two special weeks with our daughter, son-in-law, and new grandson Jack. Even though we had first laid eyes on Jack only two weeks earlier, as I sat there, waiting for lift off, I could no longer imagine life without him. During those two weeks, I learned a lot from my new grandson. Some of the lessons came directly from Jack himself and some came to me indirectly. During our flight, I tallied important lessons received from such a little person during the first weeks of his life.

*1. Having a grandchild is a privilege, not a right, an "if" rather than a "when."* At several weddings I've attended, a parent of the bride or groom has said publicly, usually during a toast to the newlyweds, something to the effect of "We're looking forward to grandchildren." Each time I heard such well-meaning but loaded words, my heart went out to the newly married couple, publicly laden with presumptions and pressure. With the percentage of women who never have children at an all-time high, there are many valid, important reasons why more couples are viewing decisions about having children not just as a *when* but also an *if.*

Nevertheless, like most women my age, I hoped for a grandchild. Up until we heard the news that our daughter was pregnant, whenever the faces of my women friends lit up as they shared stories about their grandchildren, a small ache flared in my chest. At the same time, I know firsthand what a monumental decision it is whether to have children. Not only does it add exponentially to one's responsibilities, it's very expensive, and—if we're being honest with ourselves—having kids turns life upside down and inside out. (I write these words as someone who has always found being a parent to be a deeply rewarding and joyous part of life.)

For the two years or so before our daughter and son-in-law called with the happy news, whenever Brenna mentioned anything about having children, which was not often, she placed special emphasis on *if*. After they called to let us know they would be welcoming a child into their family, my daughter explained that she had used such cautionary words with me to keep my "grandmother hormones" in check. But she needn't have worried. I have always known (intellectually, at least—the heart is another matter) that having a grandchild is not a right but a privilege. Now that Jack is here, I will and do gladly tell almost anyone who will listen (except friends who know for sure they'll never have the pleasure of being grandparents) just how sweet a privilege it is.

*2. Grandparents belong in the wings.*

As a child born to two adoring parents who love each other and him, Jack drew a lucky hand. A favorite photo from that first visit captures a moment when our son-in-law Ben and Jack, who lay peacefully on his father's thighs, mimicked each other's goofy expressions, chins tucked in and eyes wide. Another memory I especially cherish was when I entered my daughter's bedroom one day just after she had finished breastfeeding. She sat in bed, knees up, while Jack lay contently on her lap, staring into her adoring, sleep-deprived eyes. These sweet scenes poignantly reminded me that the role of grandparents is to be offstage, standing, ready in the wings, with only modest parts to play.

Our daughter and son-in-law stand center stage, firmly in charge. They write the script, and, as with all parents, it will be full of edits in the margins, some of them in red ink, because raising kids is a crapshoot no matter how many books one reads. Our job is to have faith in them, to cheer them on, and to be there, behind the curtain, ready to help ... but only when they ask for it. (This is generally a good rule for many types of relationships.)

*3. It's never too soon to start exploring the world.*
When my husband and I travel, we almost always seek out the wild places. We also prefer to spend enough days in one place to get a good feel for it. One year in Utah, we split eight days down the middle, the first four days at Zion National Park and the rest of the trip at the mystical Bryce Canyon. Only after a full three days in Zion did we feel like we'd earned the right to say we had truly experienced the place, had truly *been* there. Then it was on to three full days amidst the magical hoodoos of Bryce. This love of exploring new places is one of the things we want to share with our grandson, especially as he gets older.

During our first visit with Jack, I figured it was none too soon to encourage him to begin exploring the world, although admittedly on a smaller scale than visiting two national parks in one week. While our daughter was catching some desperately needed sleep, if Jack began to fuss, I pressed him close to me and did a small walkabout, talking to him all the while. After sliding open the glass doors to the deck, I carried him outside. During our visit, Jack often turned his head toward the windows. One theory why babies, especially newborns, look toward the light is that their eyes are unable to focus very well. Were his eyes drawn, I wondered, to the rich parade of greens from the trees and plants? The tree branches dancing in the breeze? The diffused light? Since newborns can't see very far, it was likely the light of day that drew his eyes. Although we could only guess about what he was experiencing, several times I whispered in his ear, "There's a big, wonderful world out there just waiting for you to explore it."

After a short stay, I carried him back inside. "Here's the kitchen, Jack," I explained. "This is where we make food." (His father is a fabulous cook.) "And after your Mama eats the food, she makes milk for you." Then we headed down the hall to the guest bedroom or to look out the window just inside the front door, out on the sharply slanted street so common in San Francisco. Often, we ended up in the bathroom, where it was soothingly dark. Hugging him close, I turned toward the mirror. "That's baby Jack," I whispered. "That's you." Often, it was there, in the bathroom, where Jack fell asleep in my arms.

During that first visit, I relished playing an admittedly small role in helping introduce Jack to the tiny wonders of his world.

*4. More than anything else, people (of any age) want to be listened to, want to be heard.*

As an extrovert, I like to talk. So naturally I talked to Jack a lot, but I also listened to him. Right from the beginning, his personality as an active, strong little human shone through. During that first visit, whenever he was well fed and comfortable, he loved to move his arms and legs. His grandfather and I called this his "exercise period." Whether on our laps, in his bouncy seat, or on a blanket on the floor, he pumped his arms and legs like a kid who was headed places. But he also had limits. After about twenty minutes or so of this, he would shift from busy to over stimulated and begin to fuss, signaling mom time.

One day during the visit, I accompanied our daughter when she attended a new mother's group. While there, I was struck by each baby's unique look and way of crying. Intrigued by the information I'd gleaned in a book on infant massage, in particular the authors' focus on the importance of crying as expression, I found myself listening closely to Jack whenever he fussed or cried. When he was hungry, his cry was distinctive and insistent. After his exercise period, when I would often swaddle him to keep him from flailing the arms that he wouldn't realize until months later belonged to *him*, he would cry for a few minutes as I carried him around the house, lightly and rhythmically shushing him or singing to him. Quite different from the hunger cry, that version of crying said, "I'm tired, and I don't know what to do about it!" After a few minutes of gentle rocking, his crying usually mellowed. Often, he would stare at me eyes wide open at first, but then slowly fluttering to a close as he eventually drifted off to sleep. At other times, when he was frustrated and needed to let the world know, I would talk softly to him. "Yes, we hear you, little Jack. It's good when you talk to us. We understand. When you have something to say, go right ahead and say it. That's why we're here, to listen."

*5. Singing is a special language.*
I grew up singing in school and church choirs. For many years, though, instead of singing with groups, I sang to myself, occasionally picking up my guitar to strum some of my favorite folk songs. Then, in 2011 I joined a Sweet Adelines, barbershop-style, a cappella women's chorus. Becoming a part of this chorus was like coming home to a long-neglected, important part of myself. During that first visit with Jack, singing was another important element of my life I wanted to begin to share with him. (He also has the benefit of an aunt, our younger daughter, who is a professional musician.) Without giving it any conscious thought, I immediately began creating lullabies, both words and melodies, to sing to him. What follows are the lyrics to my favorite one: *Sweet baby Jack, it's time to go to sleep. Close your weary eyes. When you wake up, your mama will be here. She'll feed you and love you and love you some more. Sleep, baby boy. All is well. You are safe. You are loved. Sleep, baby, sleep.*

Although other mammals can sing, there is something distinct in the ways we humans sing to each other. Those times alone with Jack, as I rocked him in my arms and softly sang only for him, gave me sweet memories no amount of time could fade. Right from the get-go, being with Jack reminded me of the power of song, as I watched him let my singing lull him to sleep. (After the three of them moved back to Michigan shortly before Jack's first birthday, during the next two years while our daughter worked toward her graduate degree, I took care of Jack by myself two days each week. During most of that time, I sang the same lullaby to him before laying him down for a nap, a ritual he seemed to relish.)

*6. Love is the best thing life offers, even as it brings with it the possibility of loss.*
I return now to that Sunday when my husband and I were on the plane that would carry us on the first leg of our trip home to Michigan. Because I planned to return less than two months later for another visit and, a few months after that, another one to help our daughter make her transition back to work, I had managed to convince myself it was a good time to leave. Plus,

two days later Jack's other grandparents would arrive for their eagerly anticipated turn to meet him.

So, when the plane's engines roared to life and it began its powerful surge down the runway toward lift-off, I was caught off guard by the sadness that hit the middle of my chest with a heaviness that hurt. As the plane's wheels left the ground, I felt viscerally just how big a claim that baby boy had staked in my heart.

As I gazed out the window at the changing landscape below, my tears turned the ground beneath us into an impressionist blur. Still, I carried a joy within, like carry-on luggage as light as a feather I would never put down, for I was, and am, a woman with a grandson named Jack.

## *Questions to Ponder*

- What lessons have you learned from the little people (or pets) in your life?
- In what ways is the experience of love or joy worth the risk of later losing it?
- What has life given you that you're grateful for, that brings you joy?

CHAPTER 45

# Make Your Own Cherry Blossom Festival

A FEW YEARS ago, with both daughters living far enough away so we didn't see them very often–our older daughter and her husband in San Francisco and younger daughter in Brooklyn, NY–I felt sorry for myself. When I complained to my friends, they typically replied how wonderful it was that I had two great places to visit. I knew they meant well, but I delivered my smile in reply through gritted teeth. If you have kids, and one or more of them have settled near you (which I define as anything within a four-hour drive), to my mind you have won the lottery, truly a much better prize than winning *the* lottery, where enormous infusions of sudden money tend, after producing an initial sense of euphoria, to royally screw up people's lives.

During that time, I ran into a good friend I hadn't seen in many years. Since he and I had last seen each other, his son had moved to Japan, married, and welcomed a daughter. When I asked whether he and his wife had been able to fly there to meet the baby, he shook his head. It made better sense and was more economical, he explained, for their son and his wife to travel to the States when the baby was a bit older. Until then, they were making the most of seeing their granddaughter through the camera eye at the top of a computer. I imagined how much they ached to reach across the six thousand miles between them and lift their precious first grandchild into their arms.

My friend's story was a poignant reminder for me to appreciate what I *did* have rather than feel sorry for myself from wanting even more. One of the points the Dalai Lama made in his book *The Art of Happiness* is that we generally compare ourselves to people who have *more* than we do. He then went on to say that one way to find greater happiness is to consciously compare oneself to those who have *less*, which leads me to a related story. (Dalai Lama, 22–23.) During our grandson's first year, I saw him four times, which felt like pitifully few visits at the time but that suddenly, in contrast to my friend, seemed like a lot. My friend would have to wait for who knows how long until that wonderful moment arrived.

When my mother-in-law was in the midst of a pity party, as she called it, I would point out to her the idea of focusing more on people who have *less* than we do, rather than on people who have *more.* As a woman who had outlived her youngest and only surviving sister by a good ten years (their two older sisters had died many years earlier), my mother-in-law never gave up her lament over being the last one standing. I can understand what a lonely place that must be. In 1983, when I was thirty-three, our father died in a fluke medical incident while in recovery from successful heart bypass surgery. Since cancer had claimed my mother twenty-four years earlier, our father's premature death left my three brothers and me staring up at a suddenly orphan sky, but with the good fortune of having each other.

When my mother-in-law indulged in feeling sorry for herself, I would remind her of everything her sisters had missed, and the happy events she had been able to enjoy, such as a Bar and Bat Mitzvah for a great-nephew and great-niece, fun-filled family reunions, our younger daughter's recital for her master's degree in jazz saxophone, and the wedding celebration of our older daughter and son-in-law, held under perfect blue skies late in May. Whenever I launched into one of these pep talks, my mother-in-law would shoot me a withering look. It was a dance I never stopped inviting her to join me in, and one she dismissed just as quickly with her signature flick of a wrist. It didn't help, she told me, to compare herself to other people.

I recently ran into a friend (and fellow coach) who had traveled to Japan a short time ago to visit a friend and see parts of a country she had yearned to visit for many years. She happened to be there while the cherry trees were in full bloom. One day, she told me, she and her friend walked to a nearby park. There, she said, groups picnicking with family and friends covered the earth with the blankets they sat upon, all of them gathered to savor the trees laden with their annual, glorious profusion of pink and white spring blossoms.

So many people were there that day, she added, that most of the blankets overlapped, with only thin slivers of grass showing here and there. I enjoyed picturing this immense quilt of people stretched out on the earth to honor and enjoy this annual celebration of spring.

Despite much goodness in our lives, too often we want more. We want our children to live closer to us. We want to bring back deceased family members. Yet to look up at the cherry blossoms of our lives, all we need is one small piece of ground, big enough for a single blanket, on which we can sit to be grateful for the day, the present moment. Our cherry blossoms come to us in many ways. So, my friends, let us sit; lay our blankets down; and invite others to join us. Rather than wanting more and sweeter blossoms, let us look up and treasure the ones that hang above us, whatever they might be.

*Postscript.* In 2013, our daughter, son-in-law, and Jack moved back home to Ann Arbor. What was a five-hour plane ride had become only a short drive to their home. Ah, the cherry blossoms they brought with them—an endless profusion of blooms.

## *Questions to Ponder*

- What are some of the cherry blossoms in your life that you forget to enjoy and celebrate?
- Can you think of a way you compare yourself to people who have more than you do? How might you shift that to compare yourself to people who have less?

CHAPTER 46

# Savor the Spring Flowers on Parade

COME BACK IN time with me to a few years ago on a day in May, for a walk in the woods. During many of my almost thirty years living in northeast Ann Arbor, I walked regularly on the Argo Park path near our home. As I walked the trail that meanders along the steep bank that borders the Huron River on the western side of Long Shore Drive, each year when the spring woodlands ushered in their parade of wildflowers, I observed the woods with extra care. But that year, my enjoyment was bittersweet. Since an advanced case of inoperable cancer was gradually overtaking my friend Karl's body, that spring would be his last. Because he was too ill to walk the path himself, others, including me, would need to be his eyes and ears during that special time.

The path I enjoyed sits on a hill that juts up to a lip a hundred feet or more above the river. The slow, patient show of spring begins with the delicate white petals and yellow centers of bloodroot, which grow daringly between its leaves that at day's end sheathe the delicate pale pink blooms to protect them from the cool evening air. Several years ago, when we were still in our home on Pontiac Trail, I was delighted to discover a few tucked into a corner of our next-door neighbor's house, very close to where we parked our second car. Based on what I've learned about bloodroot, most likely at one time, in that small, shaded space, some ants dropped a few seeds that managed to take hold. For many years, the lovely, fluted leaves that grew there so shyly garnered no attention except for when my husband unknowingly brushed up against them as he walked around the car to the driver's side. But after discovering them growing there, and because they bloom only a day or two, thereafter in spring I did my best to remember to watch for their blooms. In many of those years, their hooded blooms had come and gone before I could admire them. But that year I watched carefully, determined not to miss them.

Next arrived the lovely trout lilies. Close to the ground with their gray-green mottled leaves the shape of small, elongated fish, they push their way up from the forest floor. With delicate yellow hoods painted with tiny streaks of red that curl up in front, they are like shy girls with eyes cast down. As I bent to lift one up for a closer look, I could almost see a blush there. Trout lily colonies can be up to three hundred years old. Although I was sixty-three that spring, when I thought about the long history of the trout lilies, it made me feel like a girl again, as if most of my life were still in front of me.

Trillium followed, nestled in clumps further up the hill, generally off the path. Because of how early in spring they appear, wake robin is trillium's nickname, which reminds me of a fun tradition in our family. When the girls were small, they would look carefully for robins, as the day one of them spotted one would be the first day of the year my husband took them out for ice cream. These days, though, many robins winter over, usually males who stick around for as long as there is fruit to be had, who move south only when they have no choice. For robins that winter in the south, when the days start to lengthen, their hormones urge them to fly north. I knew Karl would get a kick out of boy robins flooded with hormones in spring.

Next to arrive were the light purple flowers of wild geranium, an admirably humble plant with a reputation for being slow to spread, out of respect for other species, not wanting to crowd them out. This being true, given how prolific this welcome spring flower was in those woods, they must have established residence there a long time ago. As a lover of everything purple, on my walks along the woodland path I was always delighted to see the wild geranium's first blooms.

The slow-moving parade for Karl continued with mountain rue, officially *ruta montana,* a big name for such a nondescript, delicate plant with its splay of small rounded leaves and flowers like tiny bells. On the heels of mountain rue came the white flowers of the mayapple—also aptly called the umbrella plant, as each grows a single, small white flower tucked modestly beneath its leaves.

Next to arrive were the small pointed flowers of *sedum ternatum*, the only sedum native to North America. Its nickname is woods stonecrop, possibly because it often grows near cemeteries. With rounded pale green leaves and star-like, pointed white flowers, this spring flower can be easy to miss, but I cherished it as one of the last ones in that fine parade, fading away only when its quickly greening leaves blocked its tiny blooms from the sun, causing then to wither and eventually drop.

With my mind on Karl, I was intrigued to read online that native peoples once used the red roots of bloodroot to produce a red dye, and that they also used it medicinally. Some food supplement companies, I learned, had been promoting the byproduct of bloodroot as a potential cancer treatment. Although I viewed then, and still view, such claims of alternative medical approaches with a skeptical eye, and the U.S. Food and Drug Administration had firmly challenged those claims, I yearned for a link between that early parade of flowers and a treatment for the cancer that would soon rob my friend of his life.

Only one year earlier, before his cancer was diagnosed, Karl had no idea how little time he had left. So, although I dedicated my springtime walks that year in Argo Park to Karl, I also took time to appreciate the flowers for *me*, because none of us has any idea how many more springtime parades we will enjoy on this sweet earth.

## *Questions to Ponder*

- What's one way you could celebrate the coming of spring?
- It's easy for us to take the pleasures of life for granted. What's one thing you could do to consciously savor your life?

- How might you give yourself permission to take more time for such simple pleasures as observing spring flowers?
- In a positive, liberating way, what's one way you could take advantage of knowing that you have but a relatively short of time on this glorious planet?

CHAPTER 47

# Love Being Alive

DURING MOST OF the time I spent writing this book, the Sweet Adelines barbershop chorus I'm a proud member of was directed by a woman who, during that time, lost her beloved ninety-year-old mother. At the memorial service, attended by as many chorus members who could be there to show our love and support, the chorus sang a song Annabel especially loved. One of the pastors of the church where the service took place spoke from the very spot at the front of church where Annabel had been married almost sixty-seven years earlier. There, she warmed our hearts with several moving stories about Annabel's life that revealed her deep dedication to family and to serving others. One of those stories offer what I believe is one of the most important lessons of all.

Just weeks before Annabel died, she was brought to the local hospice facility to spend her final days in as much comfort as the staff and volunteers there, along with members of her family, could provide. During the admission process, a staff member asked Annabel what her goals were while she was in hospice. (This question revealed just how much wonderful progress our society has made in helping people and the loved ones who surround them prepare for death.) Knowing full well that her remaining days on the earth were few, Annabel answered (with a smile, I imagine), "Why, to *live*." And then she added, surely without a trace of self-pity, "I *love* being alive!"

Taking a priceless lesson from this fine woman, let us remember every day to simply love being alive.

## *Questions to Ponder*

- In what kinds of ways do you already remind yourself to love being alive?
- What causes you to forget how your life is such a gift?
- What's one small thing you could do each day to remind yourself?

# About the Author

Glenda Haskell is a career and life coach, an author, and a poet. In the early 1970s, Haskell was honored to study independently with American poet Hayden Carruth, who taught her a great deal about writing and life. In 2011, she retired from a long and fulfilling career at the University of Michigan to focus on serving others and her many and varied other interests.

Haskell is the author of the poetry collection *Rebuilt Engines*. A native of Vermont, she now lives in Michigan with her husband. They have two grown children and a grandson.

## *Coaching Services*

To learn more about the coaching services Glenda provides as an Associate Certified Coach with the International Coaching Federation, visit her website at www.glendahaskell.com.

As an experienced professional coach who has witnessed the power of coaching firsthand with a broad range of clients, she is pleased to offer a complimentary coaching consultation to anyone who is ready to make important, fulfilling changes in their life. She specializes in helping professional women in mid-career and beyond to pursue career-related goals they're passionate about and to achieve other important life goals.

Glenda also serves as a registered Mentor Coach for life coaches seeking to become certified (or re-certified) with the International Coach Federation.

To learn more, contact her at glenda@glendahaskell.com.

# Cited Works

Allen, David. *Getting Things Done: The Art of Stress-Free Productivity*. New York, NY: Penguin Books, 2003. Print.

*American Time Use Survey – 2012 Results, Bureau of Labor Statistics, U.S. Department of Labor* Web. www.bls.gov/news.release/archives/atus_06202013.pdf. Accessed 6 April 2017.

Baumeister, Roy and John Tierney. *Willpower: Rediscovering the Greatest Human Strength*. New York, NY: Penguin Books, 2011. Print.

Burns, David D. *The Feeling Good Handbook*. New York, NY: Plume, 1990. Print.

Byl, Christine. "Dog Years: Who Builds Those Thousands of Miles of Park Trails and How Do They Do It.?" *National Parks Magazine*, Spring 2013. *National Parks Conservation Association* Web. www.npca.org/articles/1092-dog-years#sm.001kkgv5314bdcrpv3y2cqyyckdzk. Accessed 12 April 2017.

*Death Rate per Year table, Bureau of Aircraft Accidents Archives (B3A)* Web. www.baaa-acro.com/general-statistics/death-rate-per-year. Accessed 6 April 2017.

Evans, Mike. *23 ½ hours: what is the single more important thing we can do for our health?* Web. www.reframehealthlab.com/23-and-12-hours/. Accessed 6 April 2017.

*Fatality Analysis Reporting System (FARS)*, NCSA Data Resource, National Highway Traffic Safety Administration (NHTSA) Web. www-fars.nhtsa.dot.gov/Main/index.aspx. Accessed 10 April 2017.

Dweck, Carol. *Mindset: The New Psychology of Success.* New York, NY: Ballantine Books, 2006. Print.

Hahn, Thich Nhat. *The Ultimate Dimension: An Advanced Dharma Retreat on the Avatamsaka and Lotus Sutras.* Louisville, CO: Sounds True, 2004. Audio CD.

HH Dalai Lama and Howard C. Cutler. *The Art of Happiness: A Handbook for Living.* New York, NY: Riverhead Books, 1998. Print.

McGee-Cooper, Anne and Duane Trammell. *Time Management for Unmanageable People.* New York, NY: Bantam Books, 1993. Print.

Myers, Amy. *The Autoimmune Solution: Prevent and Reverse the Full Spectrum of Inflammatory Symptoms and Diseases.* New York, NY: HarperCollins, 2015. Print.

Prochaska, James O., John C. Norcross, and Carlo C. DiClimente. *Changing for Good: A Revolutionary Six-Stage Program for Overcoming Bad Habits and Moving Your Life Positively Forward.* New York, NY: HarperCollins Publishers, 1994. Print.

Sapadin, Linda and Jack McGuire. *It's About Time: The Six Styles of Procrastination and How to Overcome Them.* New York, NY: Penguin Books, 1996. Print.

Sisson, Mark: *The Primal Blueprint: reprogram your genes for effortless weight loss, vibrant Health, and boundless energy.* Malibu, CA: Primal Nutrition, Inc., 2009. Print.